"*Glue* offers a rare gift to project managers. It artfully blends specific step-by-step recommendations of how to move from project management to project leadership with the psychological rationale for taking those steps."

Robert B. Cialdini, author of *Influence* and *Pre-Suasion*, Regents' Professor Emeritus of Psychology and Marketing at Arizona State University

"Emerging from the pandemic, organizations need leaders who unlock the creativity and engagement of their teams by building strong, personal emotional connections. In *Glue*, Anh Dao Pham vividly brings compassionate, positive, nimble leadership to life, demonstrating with actionable guidance, the power of caring and connection to inspire outstanding results." **Peter Steinlauf,** Founder of Edmunds.com

"If you've ever led a project, go out and buy this book. It's wonderfully practical and specific, making it extremely useful. Anh Dao Pham has distilled a lifetime of experience and best practices into a guide for those who lead others in getting things done. From sticky-note roadmap meetings to ice-breaking candy jars, this book is full of ready-to-go advice that I find myself already putting to use."

Daniel Yates, Executive Chairman, Dandelion Energy, Climate Tech Investor, Founder and CEO of Opower

"No authority? No problem. Finally a business book for you, not the CEO. Glue shows the rest of us how to create and harness influence to lead an organization to success, even without formal authority."

Nick Gorton, Chief Innovation Officer of Edmunds.com

"Anh redefined the constellation of roles around delivery of complex and critical projects for me. While your first choice for learning how to become stronger at delivering projects should be to choose to go work with her, reading, absorbing, and playing with the strategy and tactics shared in this book until they are your own will accelerate your path to impact. Over a decade after starting to work with Anh, I continue to see echoes in my day-to-day activities tracing back to projects that we worked on together. Read this book, make some friends at work and go change the world."

Devin Dawson, Engineering Manager at Meta

"Anh's infectious enthusiasm for empowering teams and leaders comes to life in this engaging read that delivers the blueprint for mastering the extreme sport of project management with the clarity, insight, and impact of a true project leader."

Lisa Murison, General Counsel of Bird Global, Inc., and former EVP of Operations, Chief Legal & People Officer of Edmunds.com, Inc.

"Truly a must-read for anyone who plans to lead teams of people to get important things done! In *Glue*, Anh generously reveals the trade secrets that have made her a one-of-a-kind superstar in leading teams to perform their absolute best and smash their goals."

Eugene Park, Chief Product Officer of Edmunds.com

"Pham's Glue is a welcome break from certification-driven books on Project Management. It's a page-turning playbook on getting big things done with working professionals. Definitely read this book to get valuable insights on how to lead and inspire teams on a daily basis."

Rick Oliver, VP of Product & Program Management, Experian

"This book isn't just for project managers. In *Glue*, Anh Dao Pham shares proven methods anyone can apply to manage friction within teams, promote collaboration, drive engagement and navigate change to simply deliver results. No matter what your role, *Glue* will make you a more effective contributor in your organization."

Richard Tang, VP of Insights & Analytics at Ticketmaster, and former SVP Global Consumer Insights & Data Analytics at 21st Century Fox

"In *Glue*, Anh Dao Pham lays out techniques to support teams in a truly revelatory fashion. By itself, being excellent at rapid note-taking seems handy, but not decisive. When Anh shares how to wield foundational skills like note-taking to enable a host of other concerns—from running effective meetings to managing inter-team handoffs—a lightbulb turns on. I wish I'd had this book when I was starting my last company!" **John Fries**, Co-founder and CTO of System1

GLUE

How Project Leaders Create Cohesive, Engaged, High-Performing Teams

Anh Dao Pham

MEDIA

Published 2022 by Gildan Media LLC
aka G&D Media
www.GandDmedia.com

Contact the author at www.glueleaders.com.

Front cover design by MIGO design

Interior design by Meghan Day Healey of Story Horse, LLC

Library of Congress Cataloging-in-Publication Data is available upon request

ISBN: 978-1-7225-0533-2

10 9 8 7 6 5 4 3 2 1

———|·|·|———

For Daddy.

Thank you for showing me how to dream big.

———|·|·|———

Contents

Part III

How to Support a Project That's in Flight

Part IV

How to Make Work More Than a Project

GLUE

Introduction

"My wife is a technical project manager, so I'm going to be hard on you." I chuckle because I can hear my husband interviewing his latest project management candidate from his office. I'm not trying to eavesdrop, but I can't help but register his words when I hear him mention me. We've been abiding by "safer at home" orders due to COVID-19 for the last year, so we are always within earshot of each other.

He's a CTO for a rapidly growing tech start-up, while I'm a Vice President, Product & Program Management at Edmunds. We met at Ticketmaster over sixteen years ago when our desks were about ten feet from one another. Ironically, it's not dissimilar to our working set-up now. He works in the garage. I'm a nomad who migrates around our house or backyard with my laptop so I can get a change of scenery during my workday. Our house is relatively small, so we are never more than about twenty feet apart. We both work in tech, and we both work on delivering projects all day every day, just in different roles.

After his interviews, my husband debriefs with me. The latest candidate was an Agile advocate whose firm belief was that scrum ceremonies could solve all of their problems. Not only did she exhibit a lack of willingness to adapt her process, she also gave lengthy responses, which caused the interview to run over time despite multiple reminders that my husband had a hard stop. The candidate from the day before didn't build much rapport with him and didn't ask follow-up questions. Several others weren't assertive enough. When asked what they would do if a developer told them a project would be late, they responded that they would just update the project status and communicate it. None responded with the initiative to deliver, which is what his company truly needs. He's interviewed at least a dozen people for this role to date and is having a heck of a time finding a promising candidate.

He's not the only one. This year, I've spoken to several leaders in my network at tech companies in Los Angeles. They all have project managers on staff but struggle to get things done. They refer to their project managers as "clipboard managers," "well versed in theory," "good at following a process," but not effective at ultimately delivering projects. They yearn for a breed of people who are more hands-on, more assertive, more adaptable—those who can drive a project to completion. They are puzzled by why it's so hard to find people who fit the bill.

I see their problem. They are hiring project *managers*, but what they really need are project *leaders*.

What's the difference? I didn't make the distinction myself until just recently. I self-identified as a project manager, a role I had held for the majority of my career. I wore the title like a badge of honor, something I earned through years of practice and refinement. However, I very rarely followed the paradigms that were standardized by the project management community at large.

I read a ton of articles, blogs, and books about project management (including the *Project Management Body of Knowledge*, also known as the PMBOK), took project management courses at UCLA Extension, and attempted to apply many of those principles to my job. I found the philosophies informative and drew inspiration from them. But I always found them lacking when applied to real projects. They were too rigid, too process-oriented, too impersonal. My approach was always more fluid, more people-oriented, more adaptable. My flexibility and desire to serve teams made me successful, and I refused to forgo those principles in order to comply with a particular methodology.

I had an enlightening conversation with a mentor who changed my perception about my unique approach to managing projects. We were discussing the future of my career. I asked if he thought I'd have to shed the badge I held so dear as a project manager so I could take on more responsibility and expand the scope of my role. While I cherished the title like it was a part of my identity, he challenged whether I should label myself as a project manager at all. It was too narrow of a description. "You're not just a project manager," he said, "you're a leader."

Since that conversation, I've evolved my thinking. I realized the reason that standard project management paradigms never felt natural to me was that I always extended my responsibilities beyond management, into leadership. You need both sets of skills to successfully deliver projects.

Now I see myself as a project leader. I don't define myself by a particular title. Instead, I bring my ability to manage things and lead people to every project, regardless of the official role I'm playing. It's the special blend of those two skills that sets my approach apart from that of traditional project managers. It also explains the gap my husband is seeing in the skills of project management candidates he is interviewing. The candidates have been trained to manage projects, not lead them. And what he is actually seeking is a project leader.

What is a project leader?

In *The Servant*, a popular book about servant leadership, James C. Hunter makes a point to distinguish acts of management from acts of leadership: "Management is not something you do to other people. You manage your inventory, your checkbook, your resources. You can even manage yourself. But you do not manage other human beings. You manage things, you lead people." All projects are delivered by people. Therefore, to successfully deliver projects, you can't just manage them. You need to lead them as well.

I apply three basic leadership principles to my projects. Each piece of advice that I give in this book will echo these themes.

Principle #1: Project leaders take full ownership of project delivery

When I'm working on a project, I take full ownership of anything that needs to be done to make the project successful. That means I lose my ego, roll up my sleeves, and dig in to help wherever help is needed. My job is to do anything along the spectrum from administrative tasks to communicating goals that will inspire the team at large.

On a given day, you'll find me taking notes, testing features, chasing follow-up items, but then also working in a leadership capacity to craft our vision and communicate it to our entire project team. There is no task too small or too large for me to take on, so long as I have the capacity and skill to do it. And my work is not done until the project is a success.

In their book *Extreme Ownership,* former US Navy SEALs Jacko Willink and Leif Babin share a similar view on leadership. Whether you are on the battlefield or working in business, ownership is the key to true leadership.

They write: "Of the many exceptional leaders we served alongside throughout our military careers, the consistent attribute that made them great was that they took absolute ownership—Extreme Ownership—not just of those things for which they were responsible, but for everything that impacted their mission. These leaders cast no blame. They made no excuses. Instead of complaining about challenges or setbacks, they developed solutions and solved problems. They leveraged assets, relationships, and resources to get the job done. Their own egos took a back seat to the mission and their troops. These leaders truly led."

Traditional project managers are taught that it's their job to track status, progress, and accountability for their projects and then report on it. They are taught to remove blockers and communicate risk. However, they are rarely coached to take full ownership of the project. Unfortunately, when you lack a sense of ownership, you also don't exert the extra effort to get the job done. In contrast, project leaders feel accountable for every aspect of project delivery themselves, not just the tracking of them. And that is what motivates them to undertake every effort to see their projects through to successful conclusion, even when they face challenges.

Principle #2: Project leaders strive to bring out the best in their teams

Stephen Covey, author of the classic leadership book, *The 7 Habits of Highly Effective People,* writes this: "Leadership is communicating others' worth and potential so clearly that they are inspired to see it in themselves." The most effective project leaders I've known embody this principle. They inspire their teams by communicating to every person why they are valued. They connect daily work to a greater purpose so that each person is able to easily see how their actions contribute to collective success and aspire to achieve it.

Project leaders also strive to bring out the best in their teams when implementing governance for their projects. While most traditional project managers lean on predefined templates and standardized processes, project leaders only use processes that boost productivity for their teams. Similarly, while many traditional project managers apply Agile scrum ceremonies religiously, project leaders follow the original intention of the Agile Manifesto by valuing "individuals and interactions over process and tools." Project leaders know there are no magic shortcuts that can fix all problems for every team. As such, they take extra effort to tailor project organization to their team's needs and cast away rules that do not meet those criteria.

In this book, I share several strategies I use to customize planning and organization for my project teams to bring out the best in them. With these tactics, I'm able to reduce the overhead associated with policing processes that don't work. Instead, I can focus my time on more impactful tasks that will help my teams deliver.

Principle #3: Project leaders are the glue that binds their teams together

One of the earliest texts on project management, *Peopleware: Productive Projects and Teams*, reveals that all major issues that occur in software projects are actually human issues, not development issues. As a result, those most successful at project delivery are emotionally intelligent people leaders who focus on creating strong team dynamics.

As an example, coauthor Tom DeMarco challenges himself to explain the value of a mysterious woman whom I can now identify as a project leader. He said, "During her 12 years at the company, the woman in question had never worked on a project that had been anything other than a huge success. It wasn't obvious what she was adding, but projects always succeeded when she was around. After watching her in class for a week and talking to some of her co-workers, I came to the conclusion that she was a superb catalyst. Teams naturally jelled better when she was there. She helped people communicate with each other and get along. Projects were more fun when she was part of them."

Project leaders intuitively do everything they can to create cohesive teams. They act as the glue that binds teams together, filling gaps in process and communication wherever there is a need.

In the sports world, a similar phenomenon exists in players that are affectionately termed "glue guys." In his article on Forbes.com, *Great Teams Need Glue to Hold Together*, Don Yeager identifies these glue guys on several teams and the traits that make them particularly effective.

"Great teams realize players like Fisher, who won five NBA titles with the Los Angeles Lakers, Battier, Ross and Johnston are the glue that holds the organization together. Teammates who build each other up, show appreciation for everyone, and connect with each other are key parts of any great team."

Glue guys go beyond their predefined responsibilities. Whether their teams need encouragement, support, appreciation, or someone who just makes it more fun to work together, they aim to fill any gap they see. In essence, they use talent and care to make their teams complete.

If you ask my teammates to describe my role on projects, they will often fumble to outline it with specific tasks or responsibilities. What they do say consistently however, is that I'm "the glue" for the project. When I receive that compliment, I know I'm focusing my energy in the right tasks as their project leader.

About this book

You can buy many books on project management, and you can buy even more books on leadership. However, no other resources combine the practice of both into one balanced approach. In addition, while many books are written about leading when you are at the top of an organization, not many explain how to lead from the middle where the majority of project leadership takes place. This book was written to fill that void.

I have had the pleasure to work with hundreds of people to deliver hundreds of projects. I've done it in consulting environments, corporations, start-ups, and start-ups within corporations. I've worked on teams of two and teams of one hundred, on projects that have lasted just one day to projects that span a full year. I've learned through trial and error how to be my best at leading projects by bringing out the best in my teams no matter the size, length, or backdrop. And despite how many people I've worked alongside, you would be hard pressed to find a person who can point to a project that I personally led that failed.

And that is what this book is about. It's the culmination of the wisdom that I've painstakingly collected since I started working. It's twenty years of lessons I've learned, distilled into a few key skills that have made me successful in a craft I love.

I'm writing this book for the breed of people who, like me, seek a sense of belonging, purpose, and satisfaction in the work of leading projects.

You don't need *project manager* in your title to employ the lessons in this book. You can be any person on any team who has stepped up to take a leadership role on an important initiative. You can be anyone who is interested in learning about how to successfully guide teams to achieve a goal. Whether that interest is temporary or a result of you wanting to linger in the profession for a bit, this book will provide you with nuggets of hard-earned wisdom that you can start applying today.

In this book, I will *not* cover standard project management processes. I will not give you a generic blueprint you can follow to lead your next project. I will not teach you how to create a detailed project plan or generate a status report. I will not delineate the differences between different project management methodologies—waterfall, Agile scrum, Kanban, and others. I also won't prepare you to take the PMP exam. You can use tons of other resources to learn those rules. I recommend you review them and that you make your own judgment call on the elements from those concepts you'll want to apply to your own projects.

What I will do in this book, however, is teach you the critical blend of management and leadership skills you need to become indispensable on any project. You'll learn what it takes to be the binding agent—the glue—that creates cohesive, engaged, high-performing project teams.

I will share the methods that I've used in my own career—both to manage things and lead people—methods that have been battle-tested against real technology projects for the last two decades. These methods were born out of my experience, rather than gleaned from classroom education. They reach beyond theory into application and can be used immediately regardless of the length, scope, or phase of your project.

Since the advice I'll share stems from my own experience, the principles will work best when applied to environments similar to those in my work history. They are most applicable to technical, software projects. They also work best in matrixed organizations, where you are being asked to lead a team of people without formal authority. I have used these same skills to run personal projects as well, such as my wedding or even the project to write this book. Therefore, I know that many of the principles are broadly applicable. Nonetheless, the advice is tuned to projects that are most similar to those from my work.

The chapters are organized into four parts, each representing a critical category of skills that can be used to navigate various project phases. In each chapter, I'll share advice, philosophies, stories, and analogies to illustrate the importance of the skill. Where applicable, I refer to notable books, articles, and other media that I used in my research for this book. If you would like to learn more about these references, you may find details about them in the References section at the end of the book. Finally, each chapter also contains a how-to section that will serve as a quick reference guide to use when you are ready to apply the principles to your own projects.

PART I: How to Get Started When You Don't Know Much—Yet

The skills in this section can be applied at any time to any project. Project leaders are often designated after a project has started, when the people who initiated the project realize it will need special care or focus to hit its goals. However, leaders often feel at a disadvantage when this happens. They feel they can't contribute until they know more, but they also won't know more until they start digging into the project. This section will help you break out of that catch-22 by outlining what you can do to add value to your project immediately, regardless of how much you know from the get-go.

PART II: How to Lay a Solid Foundation for Your Project

These skills focus on work you'll need to do in the earliest phases of your project to lay a solid foundation for execution. If you're lucky enough to be assigned a project at its inception, you can start with these sections right away. Even if you join a project after it is already up and running, it's useful to refer to these sections to sanity check for steps that may have been skipped during the initial kickoff. If you find gaps, you can take a step back for a moment to apply advice from this section. When your project is moving fast, it's helpful to confirm you haven't overlooked anything that will be crucial to your project success down the line.

PART III: How to Support a Project That's in Flight

Once your project is in full swing, you'll need a few tricks up your sleeve to keep it on track. The skills in this section will teach you to navigate and overcome the challenges that arise during project execution. They are essentially the skills that you'll need to drive your project to completion, regardless of the surprises that you face along the way.

PART IV: How to Make Work More than a Project

This is the shortest section in the book, but one I'd be remiss to leave out. In this section, I share my advice for how to make your projects fulfilling.

By the time you finish reading this book, you'll have consumed the best advice I have to give to any aspiring project leader. At the end of the day, however, the secret ingredient to putting what you learn to good use is something only you can bring to the table. It's *you.*

Every project is unique. It has unique goals, timelines, constraints, unique people you will need to lead with unique personalities. You will also make your project unique because you will bring your own experience, perspective, and talents.

You will use your instincts to apply the most appropriate skills you learn from this book to meet your project's specific needs at the moments when your team needs help the most. That's how you will become the glue for your team. That's how you will both manage and lead. And that's how you will be the project leader your team really needs.

Let's get started.

PART I

How to Get Started When
You Don't Know Much—Yet

CHAPTER 1

The Magical Candy Bowl, and Other Tricks to Build Rapport Quickly

"Come to the dark side." Those were the instructions I received in the email from my new boss at Ticketmaster. At first, I thought he was making a geeky reference to *Star Wars*. But when I arrived on the third floor of the West Hollywood office, I realized he was being literal. The elevator was located in the middle of the building, with entrances to two different sides of the floor. To my left, the side that faced north had the overhead lights turned on and sun shining through the blinds from windows that faced Sunset Boulevard. To the right was the side that faced south. There, the lights were off and the shades were drawn, creating an ominously dark room to enter as a new hire. I wondered for a moment if I would be working with vampires.

"Not vampires, just engineers," joked my new boss. He explained that our website engineering team was housed on the dark side of the third floor. They were a sea of introverts with huge monitors. They enjoyed the quiet and hated the light because it made it harder for them to see code on their screens. As a result, all of the folks who shared that side with them, including my team, endured the darkness.

As I sat in the dark at my desk, I wondered how I was going to get to know my new team. It was my first job as an official project manager, and I knew that establishing strong working relationships would be key to my success at Ticketmaster. As a self-proclaimed introvert myself, I'd have to come up with a game plan to break out of my shell and break down the shells of the engineers.

A week later, while picking up lunch at a Trader Joe's nearby, I found the answer taunting me: candy. The shelves were stocked with wonderful treats—peanut butter cups, English toffee, chocolate-covered nuts, yummy sugary gummies. I drooled over the treats but knew I'd become a blimp if I ate them all myself. So, naturally, I decided to buy a tub to share with my coworkers instead. It would make for a great excuse to talk to them, while also satisfying my sweet tooth.

And so it began. Every day at 4:00 p.m., I'd walk from desk to desk to offer people treats and strike up a chat. You'd be surprised how easy it is to make the most reclusive people happier and more social with food. I learned so many details about those who would share the dark side with me for the next four years by offering them candy.

The candy breaks helped me establish rapport with my team quickly. The practice also had a few unanticipated benefits. Because I had approached my teammates first, I became inherently approach-able for future project-related questions. Additionally, my team started to see me as someone who was always giving them some-thing, rather than only asking them for something. As a result, they were more receptive when it came time for me to actually ask them for help.

As a project leader, your success depends heavily on your ability to quickly build rapport with teammates, the way I did using candy breaks. It's a role that requires you to talk to more people than any other role on your team. You will be communicating to every person with a stake in your project and asking for their help so the team can deliver. When you have strong relationships, all other project tasks are easier because your team is receptive to you. When you lack rapport, every request will feel like an uphill battle.

When I meet a new project leader, I can predict their likelihood of success based on how quickly they are able to develop rapport with me. If I end the meeting feeling distant from them, I know they'll likely be dead in the water before they even get started. If, on the other hand, I feel as if they are an old friend, I know they will likely succeed.

Now I start every project by focusing on how to build rapport. To this day, the "candy bowl effect" is one of the first tricks of the trade I use to create strong relationships. I always keep a candy bowl at my desk. (I actually always keep my teams well fed in general.) The bowl is a beacon, attracting people to stop for a treat and a chat with me. People remember who I am when they help themselves to the treats even when I'm not at my desk. "I took candy from your candy bowl!" they'll admit. Once I hear that, I know I have an ally.

If candy is not your thing, don't be afraid to try this concept with something else that is more suited to your personality. I knew a coworker who kept video games at his desk he could lend out to others, another who gave away grapefruit he had harvested from a tree at home, and yet another who baked constantly and brought her baked goods to share. Any form of giving and receiving is effective, as long as it's something that feels natural to you and allows you to engage with others.

What other tactics can you use to build rapport quickly? In the next few sections, I'll talk about a few tricks you can use to quickly build your own army of allies.

Learn names and communication preferences to make others feel important

When you meet new people, one of the simplest and most crucial investments you can make is to learn their names quickly. Using a person's name will make you immediately more personable. In the classic book *How to Win Friends & Influence People,* Dale Carnegie shares this wisdom: "We should be aware of the magic contained in a name and realize that this single item is wholly and completely owned by the person with whom we are dealing ... and nobody else. The name sets the individual apart; it makes him or her unique among all others. The information we are imparting or the request we are making takes on special importance when we approach the situation with the name of the individual." Using a person's name when you speak to them shows respect, makes them feel important, and makes them more likely to listen to you.

To use a person's name correctly, you must also learn how to spell it and pronounce it. In a multi-ethnic workplace, it is critical that you do not assume you know how to say an unfamiliar name until you ask. As an example, my first name, which is only three letters long A-n-h, gets frequently mispronounced. This is at least in part due to the fact that Vietnamese people whose families originate from different regions of Vietnam will pronounce my name differently. My family is from Northern Vietnam, and because of this, I prefer the pronunciation "Ann." When someone I meet takes the time to ask me how to say my name, I silently celebrate. Little do people know how much I loathe the alternative pronunciation of "On" and how much happier I am when I respond to my preferred pronunciation of "Ann."

A similar rule applies to nicknames. For example, I have a friend named Philip who hates being called Phil. It's the easiest way to get on his bad side. Asking him what he preferred to be called saved my relationship with him before I had the chance to unintentionally offend him. You can gain similar brownie points from any new acquaintance by being courteous and taking the time to learn how to say their name correctly.

In addition to names, aim to learn preferred communication methods. These days, we are inundated with so many ways to communicate that it's hard to choose which one to use. However, each person typically has a strong affinity to a particular method that they will use more regularly than others. Some prefer to speak one-on-one, while others are more articulate in writing. Some prefer to write long, thoughtful emails, while others like casual chatting via Slack. Some people are attached to their phones but prefer text over a phone call.

Given the number of people who collaborate remotely, there has also been an explosion of electronic communication tools. At my job, we have a choice of email, Slack, and Google Chat for asynchronous communication. For meetings, we have Zoom, Google Meet, Slack calls, and even Slack huddles. When you speak to any individual, you find that each person has favorites and corresponding pet peeves.

Using a person's preferred method of communication and their preferred communication tool is akin to speaking to them in their native tongue. If you use the methods that are most comfortable to them, they will understand you better and also respond to you more quickly. For example, my technical lead doesn't check email intraday but monitors Slack messages closely. He will respond in minutes to Slack but take at least a day to respond to emails. On the other hand, my boss doesn't use Slack much. When I send him a message there, I rarely receive a response. If I send him a text message instead, I receive a reply in minutes. That makes a big difference when I need to get an answer quickly.

I have a hard time remembering names and communication preferences, especially when I meet a lot of people at once. To help, the first thing I do on any project is create a contact list. I generate a simple spreadsheet with the names and roles for each person on my team. Then I use it to collect email addresses, phone numbers, and preferred methods for communication. The contact list is a shortcut to bypass the initial awkwardness of learning what works best by trial. Once I have a contact list, I can refer to it as needed until I remember names and preferences by heart. By then, I've already made a positive impression because I've made each person feel more important by remembering them.

Team Member	Role	Email	Mobile Phone	Office Phone	Slack Handle	Preferred Contact Method for Standard Response Time	Preferred Contact Method for Most Immediate Response During Business Hours	Preferred Method of Contact for Most Immediate Response OUTSIDE of Business Hours
Anh Pham	Product Management/ Product Lead	anh@ gluleaders. com	XXX-XXX-XXXX	–	@anh	slack / email	slack / text	text

Example of a contact list.

Be approachable to encourage others to come to you

When you lead projects, you always want to encourage people to come to you when they have concerns or questions or need help. To establish this dynamic, you need to be perceived as someone who is approachable.

The easiest way to make yourself more approachable is to smile more often. In *How to Win Friends & Influence People*, Dale Carnegie identifies smiling as the second major principle from his book. He wrote, "Actions speak louder than words and a smile says 'I like you. You make me happy. I'm happy to see you.'" Making a conscious effort to exude friendly energy using a smile can have a dramatic effect on how people react to you.

I have a friend who is always being approached by people who want to talk with her—in the supermarket, in line at the airport, even in the elevator. She has a big bright smile that makes people feel comfortable instantly with its warmth. In contrast, smiling doesn't always come naturally to me because I'm introverted. I have noticed, however, that when I start a conversation with a more serious expression, people are automatically more reserved. On the other hand, when I make the effort to greet people with a genuine smile, they immediately become more relaxed around me. People approach those who smile more often, and that small gesture greases the wheels for building strong rapport.

Another way to be more approachable is to make yourself physically accessible to your team. I've worked at companies where project leaders are seated far away from their teams, which creates both a physical and social disconnect. If there is a center of activity for your team, consider moving your desk so that you are closer to it. Your team will get more used to your presence and will have easier access to you when they have questions.

If you have team members who work remotely, consider creating a virtual space where you can collaborate. Many teams have adopted collaboration tools such as Slack or Microsoft Teams to keep conversation fluid across the team no matter where each person is located. If your team doesn't have a virtual space, seek out a tool to use and introduce one to them. Then make yourself accessible by participating actively in discussions within your virtual space.

You can set the tone for new relationships by consciously thinking about how to make yourself more approachable. The simplest way is to smile more often, but you can also make a difference with minor adjustments to body language, choosing a desk nearby, being active in virtual collaborative spaces, and giving people your full attention when they do speak to you. You will be more successful if your team is comfortable approaching you. It will lay the foundation for open communication down the line, which will ultimately make you more effective at leading your team as you get deeper into your project.

Take the initiative to be helpful

Being helpful is one of the best ways to get more socially integrated with your team. When I speak to new project leaders, they often tout that they share the same belief. However, when I dig in further, I realize they stumble on what it means to actually be helpful. "I've told them to let me know when they need help, but they haven't come to me yet," these project leaders will say. What they don't realize is that to be truly helpful, you can't wait for someone to ask. You have to be observant and then you need to act proactively based on your observations. If you see a task being dropped, you need to offer to pick it up and run with it. If you see a need, you must offer to fulfill it.

One personal example I have of this dynamic will resonate with new parents. In the first few months after my first child was born, I felt constantly overwhelmed. My husband and I would often fight because I never felt like he pitched in enough with chores. To his credit, he would always help when I asked. However, by waiting for me to ask him for help, he ultimately put the burden on me to manage him and the tasks I needed him to do. Instead of waiting, I wanted him to take the initiative to fold the clean laundry when he noticed it was still piled in the laundry basket, wash dishes if he saw them sitting in the sink, offer to take the baby when he knew I was flustered and needed a break. I didn't have the time or energy to delegate work to him. I wanted him to anticipate needs so that I didn't have to instruct him. I needed him to take the initiative to help.

Similarly, if you are not being asked to help your team, it's likely because your teammates are too busy or overwhelmed to think about what to delegate to you. Taking initiative is the key to being successful. You need to offer to help with specific needs whenever you see a need that arises so you can take the burden off the team from having to give you something.

When you are giving and being helpful, you not only establish rapport, but you begin to create a virtual piggy bank of favors that can later be cashed in. This is because humans have a natural tendency to reciprocate when they are given something. In his book *Influence*, social psychologist Robert Cialdini calls this the Rule of Reciprocation. "[The rule] says that we should try to repay, in kind, what another person has provided us. If a woman does us a favor, we should do her one in return; if a man sends us a birthday present, we should remember his birthday with a gift of our own; if a couple invites us to a party, we should be sure to invite them to one of ours.

By virtue of the reciprocity rule, then, we are obligated to the future repayment of favors, gifts, invitations, and the like."

Establishing a giving and helpful reputation with your team early will make it easier when you need to ask them to help with a task. When you are helpful to your team, they will reciprocate by being helpful to you in the future.

How can you be helpful if you don't know much about the project yet? Offer whatever you have to give and do it without waiting for people to ask. If your teammate shares a question, offer to track down the answer. If he shares a concern, help him explore options for how to mitigate it. If he just wants someone to listen to him vent, listen attentively and give him your full attention. Whatever your teammate needs, try to fulfill it to the best of your ability given the tools, skills, and knowledge you have available. If it's something you don't know, ask how you can learn it.

Show appreciation to strengthen relationships

I once received the simplest and most revealing compliment I've ever received from an engineer who worked on our systems team at Ticketmaster. The team was small and worked as a services organization; they responded to tickets that were opened by closing them as quickly as they could make their way through the queue. "It's nice to work with you," he said. "You say 'thank you.'"

Before that conversation, I didn't realize how often people forget to show appreciation when they receive help from coworkers. We are taught to say please and thank you when we ask for a favor. But when we ask someone to do what we perceive to be their job, we tend to forget. Extending this common courtesy anytime you ask for anything can go a long way to building strong relationships.

Matt Mochary, a former CEO and now coach to many Silicon Valley CEOs, identifies acts of appreciation as one of the most critical habits of effective CEOs. In his book *The Great CEO Within*, Mochary recommends showing appreciation daily to your coworkers to win them over. He says: "When you catch yourself feeling grateful about someone or something that they have done, let them know. When you hear something nice said about someone, let them know . . . The recipient will feel connected and appreciative to you for having brought them this good feeling." This habit is just as important for leaders in the middle part of the organization as it is for CEOs. Appreciation is such a simple act, but it can make a big difference in strengthening your relationships.

When you show appreciation, don't just do it generically. Your compliments will have more impact when you personalize them. When a coworker completes a task for you quickly, say, "Thank you for taking time out of your schedule to do that so fast!" When someone takes painstaking effort to explain a concept to you, say, "Thank you for being so patient with me." When a coworker noticeably goes above and beyond, praise them for their additional effort. Show them you noticed exactly what they did and make them feel good about it. Compliments are free, so give them freely. Take advantage of this simple ability to make people feel appreciated for their hard work, especially if they are taking the time to help you.

These behaviors—being approachable, giving, helpful, and showing appreciation—are a magic combination. When you start a project, even if you know nothing and no one, lean on these principles to build rapport. You'll immediately start to feel more integrated and useful. You will also become instantly more connected to your team, which will bolster all subsequent interactions you have with them during your project.

Organize team events to build team cohesion

One final, simple action can help you quickly build rapport on your team, and it works every time. You can use your organizational skills to plan team events and celebrations. Becoming the unofficial social chair, even if you know nothing about the project yet, creates a lot of positive reinforcement for your team. It also gives you a chance to get to know your team in a more informal setting, so that you can create stronger bonds.

If you're questioning whether it makes sense for a project leader to invest time in such a basic task, the answer is yes. Numerous studies have shown that the more connected people feel to one another, the more productive they are as team members. Shawn Achor, CEO of GoodThink, shares his advice based on evidence he has gathered from his years researching happiness and positive psychology. In his book *The Happiness Advantage,* he states: "The more the team members invest in their social cohesion, the better the results of their work." By taking the initiative to foster social interactions, you can improve morale and ultimately help your team improve their ability to deliver.

So what types of events should you organize? When you consider both personal and professional occasions, there are so many opportunities for teams to bond in some way. You can pick anything that feels meaningful to you to start this practice. When you kick off the project, organize a team outing so that folks can get to know one another. When a birthday comes around, buy a card that your teammates can sign and arrange a surprise birthday song. When your team hits a major milestone, organize a team dinner. When a coworker leaves the team, find a thoughtful way for the team to say goodbye.

Celebratory events can be organized virtually or in person depending on your working arrangements. I've organized many surprise birthday songs via Zoom, virtual cards using services such as Kudoboard.com, and sent meals to people for virtual luncheons using services like Uber Eats. Just keep on the lookout for a ripe occasion, then use your creative energy and organizational talents to rally your team around it. Your team will appreciate your efforts and you immediately.

HOW TO BUILD RAPPORT QUICKLY

Be giving to build allies.

- Use a candy bowl or think of another item you can give that suits your personality. Doing this early will establish you as someone who gives to your team, rather than just someone who asks. It will make them receptive to later requests.

Learn names to make others feel important.

- Capture names, roles, and communication preferences in a contact list for easy reference.
- Ask teammates how to pronounce their name and if they have a preferred nickname before you assume you can use it.
- Learn and use your teammates' names as early as possible. Your relationships will immediately feel more personal because you will establish to your teammates that you view them as important.
- Use the communication method that each teammate most prefers. This will resonate with them better and evoke a faster response.

Be approachable to encourage others to come to you.

- Think consciously about making yourself accessible and approachable to your team.
- Smile to make people feel more comfortable when you greet them.
- Move your desk to sit closer to your team.

Take the initiative to be helpful.

- Don't wait for your team to ask you for help.
- Take the initiative by offering to run with specific tasks when there is a need. This will make your teammates begin to value your contributions immediately and strengthen your rapport.

Show appreciation to strengthen relationships.

- Say thank you and share specific compliments when people help you. This will make them feel good about the work they are doing to help you and also make them feel more connected to you.

Organize team events to build team cohesion.

- Keep on the lookout for both personal and professional occasions for your team. Organizing events will improve social cohesiveness, which will in turn boost morale and productivity and garner appreciation for you.

CHAPTER 2

Be a Hero—Run Productive Meetings

I love productive meetings. They have a crisp start with attendees who arrive on time and are ready to give you their full attention. You have the right people to make decisions. The experts air their opinions and respect each other by listening. Agreement comes amicably and swiftly, agenda items are ticked off, and open items are assigned so that nothing is left to question. Time is well spent. You leave energized by the insightful talk, the collaboration, and the feeling that you are getting somewhere on your project. Within minutes after the meeting, you send a recap with satisfaction, essentially tying a bow on the whole affair.

On the other hand, a bad meeting can feel like a disease that is sucking the life out of you. Critical attendees run late or no-show. Everyone is multitasking to the degree that you wonder why they came. Energy in the room is low. Topics meander. Halfway through the meeting, someone interjects, "What exactly are we talking about here?" The meeting's end time passes. Some people keep talking, while those not participating quietly peel off to run to other meetings. No decisions are made, and you leave no further along than when you started.

My schedule contains four hours of meetings on a light day and eight hours on a packed day. On the days I run ragged from meeting to meeting, the misery of an unproductive hour is even more acute. The opportunity cost is not only my sanity but my lack of ability to do more constructive, independent work during the day. I leave these meetings frustrated that the waste could have been prevented had the meeting organizer invested more time to become fluent at facilitating meetings.

I'm not the only one. According to Atlassian, an Australian software company, the average employee spends sixty-two hours per month in meetings and considers half of their meeting time wasted. Based on a forty-hour work week, thirty-one hours a month amounts to roughly 18 percent of working time that can be better spent in the hands of a prepared meeting leader.

Moreover, there is proof that unproductive meetings affect employee morale. In a study published by MIT Sloan, "The single most powerful factor in job satisfaction was how one feels about the effectiveness of the meetings he or she attends; negative feelings were exacerbated as the amount of time spent in meetings increased. Employees who attend a rash of bad meetings are stressed, dissatisfied with their jobs and more predisposed to leave." Bad meetings are an indicator that you don't respect your attendees enough to make good use of their time. Productive meetings show respect.

Where there is failure, there is also an opportunity for you to stand out and impress people with your skill. The first meeting you run is your chance to demonstrate that you can execute well as a leader. A meeting is like a mini-project; it has a distinct purpose, a defined start time, and a defined end time. If your meeting fails to be productive, your attendees will doubt your ability to lead. In the future, they will be reluctant to attend any meeting you call. On the flip side, if you run your mini-project successfully, you will earn the respect of your project team and begin to establish yourself as the rightful choice for your role. And they will ask you to run more of their meetings.

It may feel like a curse to be asked to run more meetings, but it is actually a compliment. When your team asks you to set up a meeting, it means that they trust you. Whether you love or hate meetings, all big decisions for every project are discussed in meetings at some point in their life cycle. Meetings will be used to deliberate options before making a decision, to engage stakeholders for buy-in, and to announce significant changes in strategy. If you're asked to run important meetings, it means your team wants you to be present when critical pieces of information are unleashed.

So here is my plea to you today: While it may seem mundane, please take the time to invest in the skills you need to run productive meetings. If you do, you will boost productivity and morale for your team, establish yourself as a credible project leader, and be at the forefront of all the most critical conversations for your project. You will be part of the cure for a disease that is carelessly consuming our working hours. You will be a hero to your team and to me.

Do you really need a meeting?

On Amazon, you can purchase mugs with the slogan, "I survived another meeting that should have been an email." These products have thousands of high reviews. There is a reason that these gifts sell well: they resonate with the millions of people who have been subjected to unproductive meetings.

To prevent your meeting attendees from buying their own mugs, take a moment to ask yourself before you schedule a meeting whether or not one is truly needed. The general rule of thumb is that you should only schedule a meeting when it is the most efficient means for achieving what you need to accomplish. In my opinion, there are only three valid reasons to hold meetings:

- You want to share an update that will be most effective when delivered personally.

- You want to check in on progress, and a meeting is the most efficient way to do it.
- You need real-time collaboration on a topic to make a decision quickly.

If your topic doesn't fall into one of those categories, consider an alternate method. Nowadays many mediums of communication can be used in lieu of a meeting: email, Slack, chat, ad hoc conversations, and collaboration in documents using tools like Google Docs are options at most companies. If you feel like you need to have a conversation but can do it in under fifteen minutes, you can also piggyback off the end of an existing meeting. Only create a meeting after you've exhausted these alternatives. The practice of being judicious before you schedule can save you and your team from wasting time.

Choose a descriptive name and agenda

If you ultimately decide you need to schedule a meeting, then the next step is to title it properly and create a descriptive agenda. Please don't be that person who sends an invite with an ambiguous meeting topic and no agenda. These details do and should make a tangible difference in whether or not your key attendees will even choose to show up to your meeting.

In the book *Why Work Sucks and How to Fix It,* authors Cali Ressler and Jody Thompson recommend declaring that all meetings are optional as a part of their Results Only Work Environment (ROWE) paradigm. ROWE is a framework many large companies in the United States, such as GAP, Inc., have adopted to improve employee performance and morale.

I witnessed ROWE in action when Edmunds adopted it several years ago. At its core, ROWE provides a blueprint for employers to improve performance and morale by emphasizing employee results, rather than time on the clock. Employees make their own decisions about schedules that work best for their professional and personal lives and are coached to be judicious with their time. Since meetings tend to be a large chunk of working time, employees are encouraged to evaluate meetings on their calendar and to decline meetings that they feel won't benefit them or others. As a result, meetings without a clear purpose get very few attendees.

Whether or not your company subscribes to this convention, it's extremely useful to adopt this mindset for meetings you schedule. Think of each of your meetings as a book on a shelf, competing to get the attention of a prospective reader. Books that catch your attention are those that have a clear and concise title and a subject that is relevant to the reader. Your meetings should be treated the same way. Take the time to craft a descriptive title and a proper agenda that articulates the importance of what you're trying to achieve. This practice is not only considerate, it will garner more participation from your most important attendees and make it a more productive use of time.

Make sure meeting logistics aren't a distraction

I liken being the coordinator of meeting logistics to being the head of the homeowners' association for my housing complex. It is a thankless job. If everything is going well, the job is invisible and you are unlikely to receive much appreciation. However, if something goes wrong, everyone notices and you receive piles of complaints.

Take the time to plan so that your meeting is set up to run smoothly and your attendees can focus on discussing the important topics at hand, rather than being distracted by logistical issues. Planning meeting logistics includes fundamentals such as

- Coordinating audio/visual, seating, supplies, and even snacks if appropriate,
- Making sure you have the right people on your attendee list and that they have accepted, and

- Making sure your attendees have ample time to prepare for the meeting.

I won't belabor these points here but have provided a checklist you can use to plan your upcoming meetings in the How-to section at the end of this chapter.

Set the tone for your meeting

Recently, an executive approached me to ask for feedback on a departmental update he had just given. I hesitated for a moment, but then suggested that he consider the energy he brings into the room when he speaks. While his presentation was informative, his tone and presence brought a more somber and serious feeling to the meeting that was mirrored by the attendees. He accepted my observation graciously and responded, "I often forget that I have that type of power when I walk into the room."

In the Forbes.com article "15 Methods of Every Effective Public Speaker," Erica Cuoto from the Forbes Coaches Council identifies tonality as one of the most important tools you can use to elicit engagement. She says, "As a public speaker, you want to pay attention to your body language and your vocal cues. While good public speakers deliver effective speeches, great public speakers are actively aware of their body and their voice at all times. Use open body language and practice allowing your tone to help dictate the audience's emotional response to your talk."

Whether you see yourself as a public speaker or not, meeting facilitation is a form of public speaking. The way you present yourself in meetings you conduct will be reflected back to you. If you start with the intention that your meetings will be productive, energetic, and fun, you can use your influence as the leader to make them so. You have the ability to set the tone for your meeting with the energy level you bring, the words you choose, and your overall demeanor.

For those of you who conduct meetings with remote workers, setting the tone is particularly important because it is that much easier for your audience to tune out when they are not physically present in the same room with you. If your camera is off during your video conference, or you are quiet and reserved, your attendees will be reserved as well. In contrast, if they see you smiling and cracking jokes, your attendees' moods will be lightened, and they will be more engaged. Which mood do you want to create in your meetings?

Set the context for your meeting

During my years in college in the 1990s, the most anticipated events each week were ritualistic gatherings to watch favorite shows, most notably NBC's "Must See TV" lineup on Thursday nights. If you walked down the hallway in the dorms in the evenings, you would see groups of friends piled together in room after room, huddled around a small television to watch their favorite shows with snacks and drinks. Those were the days that birthed cult fetishes for TV shows like *Seinfeld*, *Friends*, *ER*, and, for the special few like myself, *Buffy the Vampire Slayer*. Since the TV shows would run one after another, each show would typically start with a brief recap of relevant scenes from past episodes. I still recall the excitement and anticipation I felt upon hearing the sound of Anthony Stewart Head's voice for the intro, "*Previously* on Buffy the Vampire Slayer . . ."

With the introduction of digital video recorders (DVRs) and services like Netflix, binge watching an entire series at once is now more popular than watching shows as they air. For the regular binge watcher, the recaps at the top of each episode are redundant. However, when the shows originally air, the recap is necessary to set the stage. The recap provides a solid reminder of the storyline before jumping into the next show.

In the workplace, jumping from meeting to meeting is akin to watching a series of unrelated TV episodes one after another. Starting an episode of *ER* while the only thing you have on your mind is the last episode of *Friends* can be disorienting. If you missed the last episode, you may be completely lost. Therefore, it's best to always start your meetings by providing context.

At every meeting, once you've announced you're ready to get started, take two or three minutes to remind attendees about the project, provide background on the events that led to the meeting, and then share what you hope to accomplish. After sharing that context, review the agenda briefly to confirm if there are any additional topics that need to be added before proceeding. This preview can help avoid disruptions mid-meeting and ensures you will focus on the most crucial topics for your audience with the time allotted.

Walk through the agenda, but be flexible to changes

Once the agenda is set, it's your job to guide the meeting and to keep everyone with you as you move from topic to topic. While following bullets in an agenda is relatively simple, meetings don't generally go as planned. So what causes deviations from the agenda, and how should you handle them? Let's talk about the most common scenarios.

SCENARIO 1: A key attendee is either unable to attend or arrives considerably late. When an important attendee is not present, you have the option to proceed with the group or postpone your meeting. Instead of blindly continuing, ask the group, "It looks like Mason [key attendee] is unable to make our meeting today. We were planning to cover the following topics on the agenda [list the topics]. Can we still make progress on these without him, or should we postpone?" Let your attendees help you decide if you can still make good use of their time and respect their decision before continuing.

SCENARIO 2: You notice that your meeting attendees have moved onto another topic before concluding on the current topic. In this case, do your duty and interject confidently but respectfully, "Before we move onto this topic, can we close out the first one? What was the final decision and what are the next steps we want to take?" This simple redirect will help you eliminate situations where you've sat in a meeting for an hour, discussed many topics, but concluded nothing.

SCENARIO 3: Your attendees jump to another topic that is on the agenda but is out of order. In this situation, don't interrupt the flow of the discussion to go back on the agenda unless the topic prior has some bearing on the outcome of this particular item. If a meeting is flowing well, it's better to allow it to continue to be productive rather than interrupt it. Just keep track of the topic you missed, and when the current topic concludes, introduce the topic that was skipped.

SCENARIO 4: Your meeting attendees introduce a topic that is not on the agenda. Here, you can again interject respectfully, "Excuse me, we have a number of topics we are hoping to cover in today's agenda. Would you like to continue with this topic instead, or can we move it to a parking lot?"

A *parking lot* is simply a place to "park" topics that may require extended conversations but can be discussed at the end of the meeting, or at a later date. If you are facilitating an in-person meeting, you can proactively label a space on a whiteboard or flip chart for parking lot items that is visible so that you can easily refer to it during the meeting. If you are working remotely, create a parking lot section in your notes and consider sharing your screen so that people can see the topics you've captured. Applying the tactic to move unplanned topics to a parking lot allows you to move on with your main agenda, while making others who raised the topic feel heard.

Having said that, remember your role is to make sure the meeting moves your project forward, and that does *not* always mean sticking to the agenda. You want to be flexible enough to allow for discussion on the most important topics, whatever they may be. But you also want to make sure everyone is following along. If everyone agrees they do not want to wait for a parking lot and that they would prefer to shift gears, then by all means shift gears. Just keep track of the items skipped so that you can cover them later.

End on time or early

Recall that people spend a ridiculously high average of sixty-two hours per month in meetings. No one wants to spend any more time in a meeting than needed. However, even though people will claim they want to have efficient meetings, it's common to have conversations run longer than expected because people are not good at self-moderating.

During the meeting, it's *your* role to keep the meeting moving. Watch the clock as you're progressing through agenda items. If the agenda is done, by all means, end the meeting early and give people back their time. Just because you scheduled sixty minutes does not mean you have to use up all sixty minutes. If the discussion on a single topic is running long, interject with a time-check to move the conversation along, or push it to a parking lot. Offer to schedule a follow-up discussion to tackle dangling items. Time is a valuable resource, and simply respecting it will gain you brownie points for solid leadership.

Reserve the last five to ten minutes of the meeting to recap items discussed. This is the time to confirm what you've heard and to make sure everyone has the same understanding. Going back to the TV show analogy earlier, don't leave your meeting attendees with a cliffhanger and no knowledge of when the next show will air. Be clear about what they should expect to happen next as a result of your meeting.

MEETING PLANNING CHECKLIST

Ask yourself, "Do we really need a meeting?"
- Only schedule a meeting if it's the most efficient way to accomplish your goal.

Assign a thoughtful meeting name.
- Does the title of the meeting accurately describe it?

Create an agenda that reflects key topics to discuss.
- What is the goal of the meeting?
- What topics do you plan to cover during the meeting? This is important so that attendees know what to expect.

Confirm your attendee list.
- Do you have the right people to make progress during the meeting? If not, consider postponing until they are available.

Choose an appropriate meeting length and time.
- How long will the meeting take? Have you allocated enough time to cover the agenda?
- What is a good time of day for this meeting? If it's an intense discussion, then perhaps earlier in the day is better when people are less fatigued. If you have attendees in different time zones, what is the best time slot that will allow all attendees to participate?

Plan meeting logistics so that they are not a distraction to making progress.
- Do you have all of the logistical items worked out for this meeting (virtually or in person) to run smoothly?

- ☐ For virtual meetings:
    - For virtual or partially virtual meetings, do you have the right room set up so that remote attendees can hear everyone who is speaking?
    - Should this meeting be recorded? If so, has that been set up ahead of time?
    - Do attendees have instructions for using the virtual meeting software (if needed)?
- ☐ For in-person meetings:
    - Is the room laid out well to help facilitate the type of meeting you are planning to have?
    - Are there any supplies you need to bring to the meeting to share with your attendees?
    - Are there enough seats in the room for all those to attend?
    - Do you have a projector and proper audio (if the meeting is large)?

Send out preparation work assignments in advance.

- ◆ Do attendees need time to prepare in advance for the meeting? If so, have you shared materials with them and provided them enough time to prepare?

HOW TO RUN A PRODUCTIVE MEETING

Do these two important tasks before you start any meeting.
- Double-check your attendee list.
  - ☐ If you are hoping to make a decision and the decision-maker has not accepted, you will want to reach out to ask her if she will be able to make it before you proceed.
- Confirm that prep work has been completed.
  - ☐ If your meeting requires a certain amount of prep work, have the attendees completed it? For example, if you plan to have your product lead present and he is not ready, postpone the meeting.

Set the tone of the meeting.
- Make sure to smile and speak with confidence. Bring the energy you want to have reflected back at you during the meeting.

Set the context for the meeting.
- Kick off your agenda by covering the following points:
  - ☐ What project is this for?
  - ☐ What events or discussions led up to this meeting? Who called it and why?
  - ☐ What are you hoping to achieve?
  - ☐ Does the agenda cover all of the most important topics for discussion?

Manage the agenda throughout the meeting.
- For each topic, introduce the topic or question and then open it up for discussion.
- At the end of each topic, listen for a decision or to understand the next steps.

- Restate the conclusion of that topic and then move on to introduce the next one.
- If you run into any deviations from the agenda, use a parking lot or get everyone to agree that you are shifting your focus before continuing.

End on time or early.

- Watch the clock and interrupt long running discussions if needed to move the conversation along. Don't rule with a heavy hand, but remind people of the time you have and make sure if they are deviating from the agenda, everyone agrees.
- Reserve five to ten minutes at the end of the meeting to read out action items, capture owners, and next steps.

Send out a recap within one day of ending your meeting.

- Publish a recap to all meeting invitees (including those who did not attend) to share progress from the meeting and next steps.
- See chapter 4 for note-taking tips.

CHAPTER 3

The Essential Questions to Ask to Get Any Project Moving

I find it easy to get hooked on a good detective series. Recently, I even started binge watching one on Hulu called *Elementary*, a modern take on the classic characters of Sherlock Holmes and his partner Watson, played by actors Jonny Lee Miller and Lucy Liu, respectively. I admire the quick wit of both characters, their intelligence, their powers of observation, their craving to get to the bottom of the crime. Most of all, I admire their ability to start investigations with just a shred of evidence and, through curiosity and persistence, piece together the full story to uncover the truth.

When new project leaders come to me with doubt because they feel as if they can't contribute until they know more about the subject, I suggest they look to characters from detective shows as inspiration. Detectives don't have all the answers in the beginning of an investigation. But that does not deter them. In fact, it motivates them. They use their ability to pose effective questions to suspects in order to learn. And through progressive learning, they are able to solve the mystery.

Project leaders are comfortable asking questions to seek the truth. They know that questioning is one of the few inherent superpowers of ordained leaders. I often see new project leaders shy from asking hard questions because they do not feel they have enough authority. Nothing could be further from the truth. When you take on the role to lead a project, you are simultaneously granted the right to ask questions pervasively. Like a detective, you are expected to prompt and probe so you can gain deep understanding, uncover lost details, and provoke action. Your team will look to you to ask the questions they are afraid to ask, and you will need the courage and skill to ask them.

To ask effective questions, you must be thoughtful about how you phrase them. Unclear questions can be a detriment to your project by creating commotion, distraction, and slowing progress. Effective questions, on the other hand, come with multiple benefits. According to a study by Alison Wood Brooks and Leslie K. John, reported in *Harvard Business Review*, "Questioning is a uniquely powerful tool for unlocking value in organizations: It spurs learning and the exchange of ideas, it fuels innovation and performance improvement, it builds rapport and trust among team members. And it can mitigate business risk by uncovering unforeseen pitfalls and hazards."

Asking effective questions will build your influence even further. Dale Carnegie told us, "If you aspire to be a good conversationalist, be an attentive listener. To be interesting, be interested. Ask questions that other persons will enjoy answering. Encourage them to talk about themselves and their accomplishments. Remember that the people you are talking to are a hundred times more interested in themselves and their wants and problems than they are in you and your problems." By being inquisitive, you will develop a stronger rapport with your teammates because they will feel you are genuinely invested in what they have to say.

I've engaged in thousands of discussions where I've had the opportunity to ask questions and learn what works through trial and error. Based on my experience, I've compiled a list of *the* questions I've found to be most effective to share with you. Each comes with a specific intent and word choice and should be applied in the proper context for success. In the next few sections, I'll spend some time explaining these questions and how to use them depending on your desired outcome. The consolidated list will then be provided at the end of this chapter.

Ask questions to empower others

For my first project at Ticketmaster, I was assigned to work on an internal tool to manage our projects (a very forward-thinking concept in the days before tools like JIRA and Asana, project organization tools, were widely available). The developer who was assigned to build the tool was known to be a prickly fellow. I was warned that other project managers had trouble working with him, and that he could be surly and combative at times.

In my first few conversations with him, he would pick at the details in the requirements, pointing out details that didn't make sense, and then almost grunt when he asked me how I wanted to fix them. Each time, I would go through the painstaking process of answering the question in as much detail as possible so that I could unblock him. However, our relationship didn't improve through those discussions. So during the third conversation, I tried a different tactic. Instead of attempting to answer all of his questions, I listened intently to his concerns. And when he was finished, I turned back to him and asked, "What do you recommend?"

At first, he was dumbfounded when I turned the tables on him. I realized at that point that no one had been asking him for his opinion. They just expected him to execute blindly no matter how badly written or illogical the requirements. In turn, he felt like he had no power to influence the final outcome and *that* was what had been aggravating him all this time. My question back to him was the turning point in our working relationship. He stumbled to answer in the beginning but then relaxed as I started accepting his recommendations. I won him over by listening to his opinions. We began collaborating more on solutions. He began trusting me more, and I began to enjoy working with him more.

I learned a similar lesson from my daughter when she was a toddler. At around three years old, she went through her "why?" phase. All she did all day was ask me "why?" questions that were exhausting to answer: "Why do you have to work, Mama?" *So I can make money.* "Why do we need money?" *So we can afford nice things, like our house.* "Why do we need our house?" *So we don't have to live on the street.* "Why don't we want to live on the street?" and so on and so forth. If you've ever been around a curious toddler, you know that the "why?" phase can be maddening. There is literally no end to the number of questions they can pose in a row (toddlers have more energy and persistence than any adult I've ever known).

When I was at my wits' end, I read a parenting blog that suggested a simple alternative to answering my toddler's questions. The next time my daughter asked me a question, I refrained from answering. Instead, I asked her, "What do *you* think, honey?" I could see the wheels turning in her head as she conjured her most thoughtful response. By turning the question back to her, I was actually empowering her to think rather than thinking for her.

Letting go of the idea that I had to know everything and answer every question was a huge relief for me. Whenever I feel stuck down a rabbit hole of questions, I turn to this technique to unburden myself by empowering the person asking me the questions to answer for themselves.

Ask follow-up questions to learn

As I shared earlier, new project leaders often feel hindered by their ability to contribute to an in-flight project when they don't have deep domain expertise. While it's true that deepening your knowledge will make you even more effective in the long run, you can still engage immediately by asking effective questions. Simply exchange your lack of confidence in the subject for confidence in your ability to learn it.

If your goal is to learn, the best type of question is a follow-up question. Sit in your meetings, listen intently, and when someone makes a statement that is unclear to you, ask a follow-up question. The beauty of follow-ups is that they require no prior knowledge but still have a positive impact.

I was trained to perform user research several years ago and was taught that one simple question often unlocks the biggest insights, "Tell me more about [this comment or topic]." It prompts others to speak but is also open-ended enough that interviewees have the freedom to choose the most important details they want to share. In meetings, I've since often used this phrase to uncover details that others may have missed had we continued the conversation without pausing to seek deeper understanding.

Follow-up questions also build trust because they signal that you are listening. According to the researchers in the *Harvard Business Review* study just cited, "Not all questions are created equal . . . follow-up questions seem to have special power. They signal to your conversation partner that you are listening, care, and want to know more. People interacting with a partner who asks lots of follow-up questions tend to feel respected and heard."

Ask questions to drive progress

I habitually ask three questions at the end of discussions to assign accountability and drive progress. I use them when I want to make sure that we act quickly based on recent decisions.

"WHAT are the next steps?"

"What are the next steps?" alone is the most powerful question you can ask to drive progress. These five words are so simple, but they can change the trajectory of your meeting from a waste of time to one that creates momentum. If you ask no other questions on this list, at least ask this one.

Think of the times in your life when you feel like things are moving in the right direction but then they unexpectedly stall. It's like the classic romance movie storyline where the boy meets the girl and instantly falls in love. Before he's had a chance to get her name and number, they are separated with no hope of finding one another again. As silly as it sounds, "What are the next steps?" fixes this plot twist as it prompts the budding lovebirds to exchange phone numbers before they part ways.

In the workplace, "What are the next steps?" works the same way. We have all attended meetings where we feel we are having fruitful discussions. But then at the end of the meeting, everyone nods their heads, gets up, and just leaves the room. Several days later, people try to remember what happened and realize they are confused and no one has taken subsequent action. You now have the tool to make sure that doesn't happen. Just ask "What are the next steps?" and don't let anyone leave until you've recorded the answer.

"WHO can/will own it?"

After identifying the next steps, you need to establish accountability. People often don't act because it is not clear to them that they are responsible. Asking "Who will own it?" and assigning the owner clears up any ambiguity about responsibility. It also gives you clarity on the person you will be able to ping when you need to check on progress.

There are times when I ask "Who will own it?" and get back crickets. Some people don't volunteer because of an already full workload; some lack confidence that they are the right person to do the job; some just lack initiative. When this happens, I alter the question slightly to "Who can do it?" Making this word change helps to identify who is capable of performing a task that provides options for an owner. After I know the options, I can work with the team to choose the best person to assign.

"WHAT is our target date?"

Once you have the name of a person, you also need to get a date to complete the work. To extract that date, ask for a target date rather than just directly asking, "When can it be done?" The word choice is important because people are often uncomfortable choosing an exact date on the spot. A target implies that you are both aiming to hit the same timeframe, but you are not trapping them. However, the spirit of the question and its effectiveness are the same.

"What is our target date?" is also a question that many will refuse to answer. People hesitate to provide dates when they feel they can't provide accurate estimates. Typically, this happens when there are unknowns they need to vet first. You can't fault them for their hesitation, but you still need to find your way to a date.

Instead of giving up, you can back into an answer by asking for the next step needed to make progress toward the original next step. Here's an example of typical dialogue I've experienced:

ME: "What are the next steps?"

EXECUTIVE: "I'd like to see a demo."

ME: "Who will own it?"

TECH LEAD: "I will do it."

ME: "What is our target date for the demo?"

TECH LEAD: "I'm not sure yet."

ME: "What needs to happen before we can set a target date?"

TECH LEAD: "I need to meet with my team to discuss the design."

ME: "Okay, when do you think that can happen?"

TECH LEAD: "Thursday."

ME: "Okay, so after Thursday do you think you will be able to give me an estimate for when we can conduct the demo?"

TECH LEAD: "I'm not sure yet. It depends on how long the design will take."

ME: "Okay, it sounds like we need a design first before we can provide an estimate."

TECH LEAD: "Yes."

ME: "And you won't know how long the design takes until you meet?"

TECH LEAD: "That's correct."

ME: "Can you give me an estimate for how long the design will take after Thursday?"

TECH LEAD: "Yes."

ME: "The next step is to get an estimate for the design, and then after the design is finished, we can choose a target date for the demo."

TECH LEAD: "Yes"

ME: "Okay, I'll follow up with you on Thursday."

It is always possible to identify the next step and to get a target date on that step. If your team is unwilling to give you a date, your next step is likely too big. Instead of pushing too hard, try backing into an interim step. There is always a next logical step. Your job is to extract it.

Provoke action by assigning a person and providing a reason

As a project leader, my daily charter is to identify the most efficient way to get things done. When my team raises a question to me, I aim to turn around an answer to them quickly. When they are blocked, it's my job accordingly to identify the fastest route to unblock them. When something is broken, I must push through a fix in the most expeditious manner possible.

But how can you get the right person to act quickly when you don't know who can answer your team's pressing question, unblock them, or fix the issue?

I see project leaders struggle to secure help in these ambiguous situations every day in the workplace, especially in requests made via collaborative tools like Slack. For those of you who have not used Slack, it's essentially a collection of chat rooms (or "channels") where you can go to have ongoing virtual conversations in a way that everyone who is "in the channel" can participate, if desired. In Slack, there is a feature where you can type @channel in order to broadcast a message to the entire channel. I see those tags often used by people making a request who need help but don't know who specifically to ask. "@channel, my report is broken. Can I get some help to fix it?"

If you have a highly proactive audience, you may get a response from a broad request like that. More often though, the people in the Slack channel will fail to respond to requests that are broadly targeted. That may seem odd when you are asking for help and you know there are more than a dozen people in the channel who saw your request, but it happens all the time. When no one is assigned accountability, no one takes accountability.

A well-known psychological principle called the Bystander Effect offers an explanation for why a group of people who witness an emergency may fail to respond. In most cases, it is not that they are lazy or apathetic—they are simply uncertain.

Social psychologist Robert Cialdini explains how you can use the Bystander Effect to your advantage. In his book *Influence*, he writes, "Armed with scientific knowledge, an emergency victim can increase markedly the chances of receiving aid from others. The key is the realization that groups of bystanders fail to help because the bystanders are unsure rather than unkind. They don't help because they are unsure an emergency actually exists and whether they are responsible for taking action. When they are confident of their responsibilities for intervening in a clear emergency, people are exceedingly responsive."

By applying what I know from the Bystander Effect, I've seen through my own experience that I can increase the response rate to my requests by using three specific tactics. First, I always target a specific person with my requests. If I'm not sure which individual to tag, I tag the person I think is most likely to be responsible, or at least will know the right person. "@Leo, my daily report is broken. Can you please help me fix it?"

By calling on Leo, I successfully assign responsibility for taking action, and I do it in a public setting where Leo cannot deny that he was on the hook to respond. Even if Leo is not the right person, he will respond quickly to let me know that is the case. If he does not suggest an alternative person who can help, I can ask him for one. Then I can tag that person with my question and repeat the pattern until I've found someone who will help me. It may take two or three questions before I find the right person, but by using this method, I guarantee a faster response than I would receive from a generic request.

Second, to make sure the urgency of the request is as clear as possible, I always include a date when I need the item completed. Like the questions to promote progress, the date is what crystallizes the accountability. Leo may agree to my request, but when will he do it? I will not have real confirmation that I will get what I need until he also agrees to a date.

Finally, to pack a real punch when I ask for something, I *always* include a reason for why the request is important and needs to be completed. In another chapter from the book *Influence*, Dr. Cialdini shares an insightful study conducted by Harvard psychologist Ellen Langer that involved a copy machine and two coworkers. In the study, Langer instructed participants to ask if they could go ahead of a person who was already using the copier. When no reason is provided, about 60 percent of people complied. However, when any reason was provided, compliance was boosted to over 90 percent. Dr. Cialdini suggests the key to improving the success rate was including the word *because* in the phrase.

It turns out that people inherently like to have a reason for doing things, and the word *because* often triggers an automatic response in humans that helps them justify their actions, regardless of the reason provided.

On my own projects, I give reasons consistently because I want people to understand that I have a meaningful motivation for the request, and I also want them to understand why their work will have an impact. The funny thing is that I've heard anecdotes from coworkers who have spoken to the people who respond to my requests where the "because" I originally provided is replaced. When they ask, "Why did you complete that task?" my teammates will often reply, "Because Anh said so."

By giving reasons consistently, I demonstrate to my team that I have good reasons for requests I make. That act builds my credibility. Ironically, the result is that the actual reason doesn't matter that much to them. They will willingly do the work because they trust that I had a good reason, regardless of what it was.

In a world where you might have no formal authority over the people you need to help you with your projects, providing a reason and doing so consistently can have a dramatic effect on whether or not people will do what you ask them to do.

For example: "@Leo, this report is broken. Can you please look into it within the hour? I'm asking *because* our CEO would like to see this report before noon today so that he can decide how much we need to spend on our next project." Now that is a request with a reason that will spur fast action.

Make statements to get a response

When I was working on projects for Ticketmaster in West Hollywood, I was assigned to several projects that required us to work with a team in a separate office. The Phoenix team was responsible for a back-end system called "the host," which was the original technology platform that powered the ticketing terminals when Ticketmaster first came into existence in the 1970s. While the team had a reputation for strong technical expertise, collaboration was often a struggle. Not only did they program in a different language than our web development team, it sometimes felt like they spoke a different language.

I experienced the communication gap fairly quickly during my first project with them. My team was responsible for building the front-end website and had informed me that we were blocked while we were awaiting direction from Phoenix on the host implementation. Several emails with inquiries had been sent with no clear answers.

To help unblock my team, I worked with our developers to understand the gaps and get their guesses on possible solutions. Then I crafted an email to Phoenix to see if I could extract a response. In the emails my team had previously sent, they had posed open-ended questions such as, "How should this work?"

Instead of repeating the open-ended inquiries, I took the time to try to answer the questions myself based on information I had gleaned. I stated our assumptions: "In order to complete this project, our team will do (A) and when they are completed, they will hand this to your team and you will do (B). We will be moving forward with this plan tomorrow, please let me know if I've misstated anything." To my surprise, they answered the email within five minutes and corrected my response with the appropriate steps. We finally had clarity on what needed to happen next.

When I reflect on why making statements works, it reminds me of a passage I read in *The Happiness Advantage*. In his book, author Shawn Achor recommends that when you are working to establish a new habit, you find ways to reduce the friction to performing that new habit. His advice, "Lower the activation energy for habits you want to adopt, and raise it for habits you want to avoid."

As an example, if you want to go to the gym in the morning, lay out your clothes and shoes at night. When you wake up, the decision to go to the gym has already been made for you, and there is no question about what is supposed to happen next. This strategy reduces the cognitive burden that you have in the morning when you have less capacity to make decisions and therefore makes it more likely that you will follow through with your plan.

Making statements works the same way. Because open-ended questions require significant effort to form a thoughtful response, it is much harder to get someone to craft that response. This is especially true when the person you are asking has little time or brain power to respond to you. The Phoenix team was always busy with work and, therefore, was less likely to respond quickly to open-ended requests for direction. Correcting a set of assumptions as I had posed, on the other hand, required much less effort on their part. And that is why we had received a response from them so quickly.

The one catch with this technique is that you must be willing to put your ego aside. You must not feel embarrassed or uneasy about making incorrect statements. Instead, have confidence that you will be able to successfully extract the missing information your team needs and that your clever approach will be commended.

THE MOST EFFECTIVE QUESTIONS TO ASK

To learn and build rapport, ask follow-up questions that empower others.

- "Tell me more about—"
- "What do you recommend—"
- "What do you think—"

To drive progress, always ask "What are the next steps?"

- For each step, ask:
  - ☐ Who will do it? *or* Who can do it?
  - ☐ What is our target date? *or* When will you know enough to provide a target date?

To provoke action, ask directed and clear questions that include a target date and reason.

- Who: Address a specific person.
  - ☐ If you don't know who, choose the most likely person who can answer.
- What: Explain exactly what you need.
  - ☐ Be clear about what you need so that it is easy for someone to respond.
- When: Provide a requested completion date.
  - ☐ If you can provide a reason for the target date, include it.
- Why: Tell them why it's important.
  - ☐ If a person who has more authority than you is requesting it, include their name in the request.

To get a faster response, reduce the work involved with responding.

- Make statements that can be corrected.
- Make it as easy as possible for people to respond to your question or request.

◆◆◆

CHAPTER 4

The One Skill I'm Always Asked to Teach (It's Note-Taking. Yes, Really!)

You will be hard pressed to find a person who is more enthusiastic about note-taking than I am. Virtually any coworker of mine will tell you that great note-taking is one of my most remarkable traits. That is no mistake. It's a skill I've practiced at length since college, since I learned how to type fast. And it's a skill I've benefited from every day at work, in every productive meeting I've run.

My ability to rapidly take great notes has been so foundational to the success of my career that I'm devoting an entire chapter to the subject.

What does it mean to take *great notes*? Great notes are not necessarily detailed. They do not regurgitate conversions in excruciating detail. And they are not hoarded from your team. On the contrary, great notes capture the most relevant points from a discussion. They are accurate, organized, succinct, and express concepts clearly. They document follow-up items with precision. Most importantly, they create transparency because you broadcast them on the heels of every important conversation.

If you take great notes, you will make a fantastic first impression. One of my coworkers once told me that he was so impressed with my notes after his first set of meetings with me that he went home and told his wife, "You should see these notes. They are better than the meeting!" Another coworker shared that if there was one thing that he would want me to teach, it would be how to master *this* skill. In fact, the other day he sent me a Slack message just to thank me for sending out a thorough recap I had typed up for a meeting he was unable to attend: "I actually had a thought about trying to coin a new acronym when I was reviewing the log. AWH—Anh Was Here."

If you know how to take great notes, you will be able to capture important information on your projects with ease. Notes are often the only system of record for important decisions for rapidly moving projects, when formality is traded for speed. When you share those notes, your teammates see you as a reliable source of important information. You become the expert they can ask later for that information.

Finally, taking great notes will help you learn new subjects quickly. I often get complimented on my freakishly good memory. However, it is not my memory that is sharp, but my ability to learn as I go. Benjamin Franklin said, "Tell me and I forget. Teach me and I remember. Involve me and I learn." Taking great notes involves me in discussions in a way that crystallizes learning on the spot. As a result, my recall ability for the details I've written is stronger than others who participated in the same discussions.

Sadly, I've met many project leaders who do not take great notes. I've heard complaints about meetings where the facilitator slowed conversation down, failed to track follow-up items, and didn't send proper recaps. I've seen important information slip through the cracks because no one took the time to document it. That is an unfortunate result when miscommunication can be so easily prevented.

Let that not be you. If I have convinced any tiny part of you of the importance of great note-taking, please read on.

Type very fast to capture information on the fly

I type about eighty words per minute, and I recommend that you aim to get your typing speed above seventy. If you are below seventy words per minute, work on increasing your typing speed. I've given this advice multiple times to aspiring leaders I've known, and unfortunately most of them have failed to take the initiative to follow it.

People who type slowly often let their egos get in the way and resist improving this skill. They see typing as a skill that is beneath them, that of admins rather than leaders. What these project leaders don't realize is that they are throwing away opportunities to establish themselves as credible subject matter experts when they relegate note-taking responsibilities to others.

Improving your typing speed is one of the wisest investments you can make. Let go of your ego and take the leap to improve. This single investment will pay big dividends over the course of your career.

If you type slowly and people see you type slowly, they will perceive it as a reflection of your intelligence. Think about a time when you've ever had to watch someone else type something and they did it slowly. Did you think they were smart? Or did you sigh and try hard to wait patiently while they finished recording the thought? Have you ever been in a meeting where the meeting facilitator typed slowly while trying to record decisions? Was it an efficient meeting or did you feel like they slowed everything down? You do not want to be perceived this way.

If you speed up your typing, you will get more done every day. I estimate that I spend 80 to 90 percent of my work hours in front of the computer and most of that is while typing. If you type only forty words per minute and spend time increasing your typing speed to sixty words per minute, you will improve your efficiency while in front of a keyboard by 50 percent. People tell me they always wish they had more time in their days. Improving your typing speed is literally a way for you to get more time in your day.

Finally, it does not take that long to improve your typing speed. There are tons of resources available to you (games, fancy programs, and books) that you can choose to improve your speed. If you dedicate an hour a day for the next ten days to improve your speed, that's an investment of ten hours. If you increase your speed while in front of a computer by 20 percent, and you spend only five hours a day typing on a computer, you will make back this time in ten days. These are long-term benefits to your productivity for a relatively small investment of time.

I feel lucky that I invested in my typing speed when I was only eighteen. I came home from college at UCLA for the summer and decided to apply for work through a local temp agency. During the application process, I was required to take a typing test so that they could report typing speed on my résumé. On my first attempt, I scored only forty words per minute, which the agency told me did not hit the bar for anyone hoping to get placed quickly. I took the hit to my ego. Then I went home determined to come back in a few days to get a better score. I was lucky that my mom already had a speed typing book that I could use. I spent about six hours practicing from her book. Two days later, I retook the test and received a score of sixty wpm. I will never forget that the six hours I invested in improving my typing speed has benefited me *every minute* that I have spent on a computer since that moment.

The original book I used is no longer in print, but I don't think it's the method that matters. You can use any method and get the same result. It's the effort you put into improving your speed that matters. Just take the time to take *any* typing test to assess your current speed. Choose *any* program that appeals to you (look online) and allocate some time to it for the next ten days. Know that it is a worthy investment of your time, and you will be amazed at the benefits you reap for the rest of your career.

Fake it till you make it

Once you type at a reasonable speed, you can use that skill to capture information. To capture information well, you must be able to take accurate notes. Unfortunately, it can be challenging to take accurate notes when you don't know the subject matter well. However, that is an entirely surmountable problem.

The key to taking notes when you don't fully understand what you are hearing is to make sure you parrot back key phrases that are being used by the people in the room. The important part is not that it makes sense to *you* in the "fake it" stage, but that you are capturing notes in words that make sense to *them,* the people who will read your notes.

I vividly remember the first time I sat in on a meeting with our advertising teams when I was asked to help on a project that had high visibility. If you have ever worked in digital advertising, you know that there is a lot of ad-specific jargon that no normal human has ever heard before or can reasonably comprehend. Even though I'd worked at Edmunds for several years, I felt completely lost in those first meetings.

What I later learned that helped me understand why it was so confusing was that the same ad unit can be referred to in multiple ways—by size, by placement, by targeting criteria, or by advertising tactic. Imagine how difficult it is to understand a conversation where the "300 x 250," the "right rail ad," and the "conquest ad" all mean the same thing. Still, when I recapped the meetings, the attendees found it helpful because the words I wrote made sense to them.

I want to be clear that capturing key phrases and parroting them back to your audience does not mean you should write down everything people say. I am not advocating that you record each word verbatim. The biggest mistake I see note-takers make is that they try to write down every word said and therefore fall behind. Even if you type eighty words per minute, you cannot capture every word that is spoken.

Great notes don't capture everything; they capture what's most important. Your role is not to be a court reporter who records everything that everyone said. Your job is to capture only what is important—namely (1) decisions that were made and (2) action items that need to be taken and who is assigned to those actions. So when you are in your meeting, these are the items you want to focus on while you listen. These are the items to record.

HOW TO FAKE IT UNTIL YOU MAKE IT

Capture the meeting agenda and list of attendees.

- Prepare the meeting agenda and attendee list for your recap before your meeting. If you didn't organize the meeting and don't understand the agenda, reach out to the organizer to get this snippet. It will help you frame the conversation.

Capture decisions that are being made.

- Listen for affirmative phrases like "agreed" or "let's do that" or "sounds good," in particular by the most senior people in the meeting.
- As you hear these phrases, interject and ask, "Did I just hear a decision? If so, can someone please summarize for me?" Then capture that snippet. People in the meeting usually find this type of question helpful as it helps bring clarity in the moment, and it also gives you a more succinct summary to capture in your notes.
- Mark these uniquely in your notes so that they are easy to find while skimming (for example, "DECISION: We will move forward with option B.").

Capture action items.

- When you hear someone asking to have something done, or someone agreeing to take on a task, capture that as an action item.
- There also will be times when you don't know everyone in the meeting or didn't hear who would take the task. When this happens, capture the action item, put a question mark next to the name, and then wait until the end of the meeting to capture the name of the owner.

⬥ Mark action items uniquely for easy skimming (for example, "ACTION ITEM: Doug will speak to Martin to confirm approach.").

Read out your summary of the meeting and fill in the blanks.

⬥ At the end of the meeting, say, "I'd like to quickly summarize the meeting before we finish." Once you get people listening to you, read the decisions and action items you've captured out loud and allow people to correct you.

⬥ Correct your notes, making sure to use the same phrases that they have used and add action items that people call out that you have missed.

⬥ For any action item that doesn't have a person's name next to it, ask who is responsible for getting it done. Capture their name and move on until you make it through your list.

⬥ When you are filling in the blanks, reread the action items again and then ask, "Is there anything I missed?" When everyone agrees you've properly captured the most important items in the meeting, you've done a respectable job faking it.

Send out your recap within one day of the meeting (the faster the better).

⬥ No one will benefit from your hard work unless you share your recap with others. Send your recap out in close proximity to your meeting, no later than one day after it occurred. The closer you can get in proximity to the meeting, the better. The longer you wait, the more likely some of your information will be outdated.

⬥ Unless it's a short list of notes, move the notes to a separate doc and then copy the follow-up items *directly* in the body of the email. People don't tend to read the full recaps unless they are looking for something specific. They also will skim recaps for their name so that they know what they need to do next.

Organize information in real time to crystallize learning

Faking it is fine for a period of time, but it should only be a temporary solution while you deepen your knowledge. You master note-taking when you can take robust notes *and* you can organize the information in real time. This is how you simultaneously learn about your project while you are adding value to it. However, it is a hard skill to learn and takes practice. You will only want to try these tactics once you have developed your typing speed, know the names of all the people on the project, understand their roles, and have a solid understanding of the objectives for the meeting and a strong grasp of the terminology.

I started developing my note-taking skills when I was in college and a math major at UCLA. Mathematicians are known to be highly methodical and also well-practiced problem solvers. However, we are also inherently lazy, so we are always looking for more efficient ways to do things. It's the reason why there are so many symbols in math that can be used as abbreviations for words. Mathematicians never write the words *delta* (Δ), *integral* ($\int$) or *summation* ($\sum$). We have an equivalent Greek letter or symbol that we use as shorthand.

At the height of my mathematical laziness, I had the good fortune to read an article in a magazine about taking notes in outline format and the benefits of doing so. Structured note-taking essentially allows you to triple-process the information you are receiving simultaneously: first you are hearing it, then you are processing it as you reorganize the information, and finally you are writing it down. As a result, you learn much faster when you are doing structured note-taking than you would by typing the words you hear verbatim.

When you are merely transcribing, you fail to retain much. You're so focused on capturing the words that you don't actually take the time to listen, and they literally go in one ear and out the other. At best, you will capture and retain only a small fraction of the information, depending on how effective the people in meetings are at conveying their ideas verbally, visually, or through some sort of demonstration.

When you listen, participate in the discussion, and then summarize the information in your own words as if you were to have to teach it to someone else, you increase your recall ability significantly. In a meeting when I take great notes by reorganizing on the fly, my recall of the information is much higher than anyone else's in the room. That's because I am processing the information multiple ways: passively by listening, actively by asking questions, and then finally by capturing what I've learned so that I can teach it to others later.

After reading the article in college, I started attending my lectures and taking notes consistently in outline format. When I did this, I learned more than I did before with normal note-taking *and* reading my textbooks combined.

Ever since college I've practiced this skill whenever I've needed to learn from a discussion or lecture. By the end of any meeting, I often have a fully organized document with key action items that I can send out within minutes of the meeting completion. It allows me to learn as I go, capture important information as a resource for everyone else, and also have extremely timely communications.

Even with the amount of practice I've had taking great notes, there are still instances when I'm unable to fully reorganize my notes during a meeting. This can happen for any number of reasons: when I'm having computer difficulties or have forgotten my laptop, when I have a particularly fast talker in the discussion, or when I am doing a significant amount of talking myself during the meeting. In these cases, I jot down a few words for each key point so that I have enough of a scent of the conversation to trigger my memory when I review my notes later.

At the end of the meeting, I make statements out loud to recap and confirm my understanding. Then as quickly as I can after the meeting ends, I take a few minutes to flesh out my notes to share with the meeting participants. You can use this same tactic while you are learning this skill. As long as you are reorganizing the information in your own words, it will be just as effective for solidifying your understanding of the material.

Capturing information rapidly through great note-taking will make you a more credible project leader for your teams. When you do it well, you will impress people with this simple act. You will immediately add value to every discussion, quickly become a hub of information for your project, and simultaneously improve your knowledge about the project such that you can be more effective with every other tip that I give you in this book.

Examples of Various Stages of Notes

EXAMPLE 1: The Worst Notes
The worst notes are no notes at all.

EXAMPLE 2: Bad Notes
Bad notes will capture most words verbatim but make it difficult for a reader to determine the most important takeaways and follow-up items.
Paul: What's your budget?
Anh: We haven't decided yet.
Derrek: We have a list that we want to work on first.
Paul: What is on the list?
Derrek: Here's the list.
Paul: I'm not sure I can do that for the budget. I have some plans I can share.
Derrek: Who will oversee the construction?
Anh: Should we settle on budget?

EXAMPLE 3: Good Notes
Good notes will capture key decisions and follow-up items.
Meeting Title: Discuss Home Renovation Budget and Responsibilities

Meeting Date: 12/7/2021
Attendees: Anh/Derrek (owners), Paul W. (construction), Paul D. (architect)

Key Decisions
- Overall budget will be no more than $xxx.
- Paul W. will be responsible for all construction materials and permitting.
- Owners will be responsible for cost of fixes.
- Paul D. will oversee construction.

Follow-Up Items
- Paul W. can provide the prices for windows & doors.
- Paul W. / Paul D. will work together to augment the original fixtures list.
- Paul W. to update plans to reflect the change in size for the 2nd bedroom window.
- Paul W. to work with Anh/Derrek to provide an estimate on the work for the garage.

EXAMPLE 4: Great Notes
Great notes will summarize the conversation in your own words and capture the most relevant discussion points, key decisions, and follow-up items.

Meeting Title: Discuss Home Renovation Budget and Responsibilities
Meeting Date: 12/7/2021
Attendees: Anh, Derrek, Paul W. (construction), Paul D. (architect)

Key Decisions
- Overall budget will be no more than $xxx.
- Paul W. will be responsible for all construction materials and permitting.

- Owners will be responsible for cost of fixtures, over the budgeted cost.
- Paul D. will oversee construction.

Follow-Up Items

- Paul W. can provide the prices for windows & doors so that we can review them and understand if there is any item that seems overly expensive before they are ordered.
- Paul W. / Paul D. will work together to augment the original fixtures list with price ranges that are included in the overall budget.
- Paul W. to update plans to reflect the change in size for the 2nd bedroom window for owners to review.
- Paul will come on Tuesday 12/19 @ 10:30AM to share revised proposal.

Discussion Notes

Understanding costs/pricing associated with choices

- Overall budget is at $xxx.
- Owners would like to understand the separate budget around fixtures/design choices to understand where cost savings are possible and when we are going over our budget with our choices. Specifically, owners would like to understand the pricing for windows and doors.
- All agree that we will meet periodically for each of the choices around finishes and fixtures. Paul W. will provide options for us to choose from and we will discuss impact to the budget.

Work Schedule

- Owners would like the work on creating the plans to submit to the city to start as soon as possible. Paul W. will be responsible for permitting process and cost.

- Reviewing the prices for windows & doors should not be blocking this work.
- Owners may make changes to the operating features of the windows but will not likely change the sizes.

Plan Updates—2nd Bedroom Window

- Paul W. will update the size of the window to be centered in the 2nd bedroom and be a larger, more typically sized bedroom window.
- Paul D. recommends owners look at a drawing of the window & size before approving.

HOW TO ORGANIZE INFORMATION IN REAL TIME

Learn how to type very fast.

- Do not attempt to organize your information in real time with your note-taking unless you type very fast. You need to be able to keep up with your meeting and to capture the most salient points without slowing down the discussion.

Type on the computer that is most comfortable for you.

- I type the fastest on my own laptop and am most comfortable navigating quickly on it, which is why I bring it with me for note-taking. I also find that people tend to make more mistakes when they are typing if people are watching them type up on a big screen and in particular on a computer they are not used to using. Typing on my own computer makes me feel as if I'm less exposed while I'm typing.

Show your notes while you type them.

- Projecting your notes on the big screen (if you dare) helps keep everyone in the loop on what is happening during the meeting and also allows people to see if what you are capturing accurately reflects what is being discussed and allows them to correct anything that you may have misstated as you typed. If you are working at a company with remote attendees, it will also help them stay engaged with your meeting.

Start your notes with a bullet of agenda items.

- These are pre-formed headings for each discussion topic. If a new topic is added to the meeting as you go, add it as a separate heading and capture notes underneath instead of trying to retrofit your agenda. You can delete or rename headings to better reflect the topics of discussion once the discussions are finished.

Don't try to write everything verbatim.

- Paraphrase the conclusion verbally or have someone else paraphrase the conclusion at the end and then type only that. This technique will also help keep everyone in the room on the same page before you close out a topic and move on to the next one.

Organize information under appropriate headings, not according to time.

- Meetings often meander back and forth between subjects and topics. Don't record them in the order in which they were discussed. Instead, record them under the heading that is most relevant. If you are taking your notes in outline format or some variant thereof, put relevant points as sub-bullets against the major topics where they are most applicable.

Capture action items in a separate section.

- Capture all the action items in one section at the end of your document rather than integrated throughout it. This makes it much easier to recap the meeting and track the outstanding items that need to be tackled following your discussion.

CHAPTER 5

Every Successful Leader Synthesizes Information—You Can Too

A few years ago, I was able to prevent two important projects from colliding. I was working on an initiative at Edmunds to redesign the advertising footprint for our website. We were working hard and testing different ad options for one of our highest-revenue-generating pages. We were making slow, steady progress. In the middle of the project, I was invited to a meeting to review an update from another team whose broad goal was to improve the customer experience on our site.

To my surprise, I learned they were planning a redesign of the same page we had been testing, and that the two projects were slated to launch under the same timeframe. When I realized the impending doom, I surfaced the risk immediately. Luckily, it was still early enough for me to work with the executives and teams to realign goals so that we could launch on time and meet both objectives. Playing a role where I was able to synthesize information, identify a risk that no one else saw, and work to mitigate that risk across disparate teams and conversations was key to the success of both projects.

Synthesis is a natural culmination of the skills you've developed to this point and is, therefore, the most mature and valuable skill. Practicing synthesis transforms you from a supporting pillar to a foundational one. It is the first skill that makes you uniquely indispensable to your project.

With productive meetings, you are positioned to be present when critical information is shared. By tuning your powers of inquisition, you are enabled to expose supporting details that others may have missed. Then, through taking great notes, you can capitalize on the importance of those details by recording them before they are lost. Synthesis is the next phase of your evolution.

According to the dictionary, *synthesis* is defined as the "combining of separate elements or substances to form a coherent whole." When you actively practice synthesis, you blend everything you've acquired into your body of knowledge with one special ingredient—you. You add your thinking to form new extrapolations and applications. Your contributions are no longer just a distillation of facts. Instead, you begin to bring fresh insights to the table.

I synthesize information daily, by continually connecting what I gather from my discussions with different people across conversations. A coworker of mine, who has partnered with me on a number of large projects, recently shared his opinion about how I synthesize: "You have a desire to understand. Instead of just running each project like you're following a pattern or formula, you try to understand the situation, the problem(s) to be solved, the true goals/mission/purpose, the people and their individual (and often conflicting) goals . . . the discovery happens as you're executing, and every bit that you learn along the way then shapes how you approach the execution. And what ends up happening is that your curiosity leads you to becoming the most knowledgeable person on the entire team—you've learned the strategy side, the business side, the tech side, the creative side, and the analytics, and you've become the epicenter of everything that is happening with the project. This is a hard (maybe impossible?) trait to teach and transfer to someone else, because just being curious is not sufficient. You also have to have the brain that can assimilate all the information and then connect all the dots."

When I synthesize information across all the moving parts on a project, I am able to provide valuable guidance to my team that cannot be provided from those who work in siloes. Using a broad purview, I can clearly see whether we are on a solid path or if the terrain ahead is littered with trouble. I can prepare my team to face and overcome whatever lies ahead.

Every successful leader I know synthesizes information well, but it is rarely taught or discussed as a skill. However, synthesis is a skill that can be developed with practice. In this chapter, I'll distill how I synthesize information into a few tangible methods that you can start practicing today.

Deepen understanding by inferring information

Surprisingly, one of the best and only texts I've found that describes how to synthesize information comes from a grade school reading lesson. In *Reading with Meaning*, Debbie Miller likens the act of synthesis to throwing a stone into a pond. "As you read, your thinking evolves as you encounter new information, and the meaning gets bigger and bigger, just like ripples in a pond." Synthesis, done correctly, progressively widens your thinking as you learn more about a subject.

Miller's lesson plan for teaching synthesis starts by having "readers monitor overall meaning, important concepts, and themes as they read, understanding that their thinking evolves in the process." You should accept that your thoughts on a subject change as you learn more about it. Next, "readers tell what they have read as a way of synthesizing." Paraphrasing what you've learned in your own words allows you to confirm that you correctly understand what you heard to date.

Finally, "readers extend their synthesis of the literal meaning of a text to an inferential level." Once you have a firm understanding of the concepts, you are then challenged to infer something that has not already been stated aloud. It's that inference that unlocks the power that is hidden in that pile of information. If your conclusion is right, you will know you fully understand what you've learned and also garner new meaning from it.

Synthesis through inference can be performed with the same steps on your projects. You listen with an open mind. You summarize what you've learned in your notes. Then, if you are brave enough, you can go one step further and draw conclusions. Here are a few simple examples to illustrate how it's done.

EXAMPLE 1:
- Dad says, "It's cold outside."
- Son says, "I want to go play outside."
- (Synthesis) Mom says, "You need to take a jacket before you can go play outside."

EXAMPLE 2:
- Martin says, "I'll be on vacation next week."
- Maria says, "I need Martin to complete this task within the next week or else I will be blocked."
- (Synthesis) You say, "It sounds like Martin will either need to finish his task this week. If that's not possible, we will need to transition his work to another person so that it doesn't block Maria."

Here you inferred that the work needed to be transitioned in order to be completed—a detail that was missed in the first two statements. This type of synthesis is even more impactful when you are able to connect conversations that take place at different times and places but are interrelated. For example, if Martin mentioned his vacation in your morning scrum and is not in the meeting later when Maria says she needs his work to be done, you can be the glue that connects those facts together.

Sequence information to identify gaps

I come from an Asian household where cooking recipes are never written. They are all done from memory and taste. When I'm craving comfort food, I call my mom to get a recipe for dishes she cooked from my childhood. On the phone, she'll typically rattle off the ingredients and instructions from memory. I'll ask her a few clarifying questions. Then once she's done with her first pass explaining the recipe to me, I'll try to repeat the instructions in order back to her. This is my act of synthesis. I combine the ingredients and instructions into chronological steps that make the recipe easy to follow. It's often during my summary that I realize we missed an important step.

This is the most common way I synthesize. As I collect information, I begin to sequence it; I write out numbered steps that I can use to explain the order in which tasks will take place. This method helps me see if I've missed a critical step in my plans.

EXAMPLE 1: How to cook chicken pho

- **Step 1:** Grill your onions and ginger and slice carrots and daikon.
- **Step 2:** Place a whole chicken into a pot with chicken stock, water, fish sauce, and star anise.
- **Step 3:** Boil for 40 minutes. When the chicken is done, the juices will run clear when pierced by a fork.
- **Step 4:** Debone the chicken.
- **Step 5:** Add cooked pho noodles to a bowl and place deboned chicken on top. Spoon hot broth over the noodles and chicken. Serve with Sriracha sauce, fresh lime, and herbs.

When the recipe is written out this way, I realize I have no idea what happened to the vegetables, ginger, and onions I grilled and sliced in step 1. Did they ever get used? (If you're curious, I invite you to visit my website at www.glueleaders.com/recipes for the full recipe.)

EXAMPLE 2:

- Martin says, "The back-end work for this story will take two days."
- Maria says, "The front-end work for this story will take three days."
- (Synthesis) I say, "It sounds like the total time it will take to complete this story is five days. Is that correct?"

In the second example, I assumed based on prior experience, that Martin's and Maria's tasks were serial. Then I tried to sequence them in order to obtain the total development time. You can see how it would be possible that the conclusion I drew was incorrect. For example, if Martin and Maria agreed that their tasks could be done in parallel, then the work would span fewer days. Another way in which my synthesis could have been wrong is that I assumed that Martin and Maria had only two tasks to complete the development. Martin might have interjected to let me know that he wouldn't be able to start until Lee has completed his database work. Lee's work would tack additional time onto the estimate.

Your conclusions don't always have to be right; the most important point is that you do the work to synthesize. Even if you are corrected, working to piece together information and applying that information to uncover new insights will deepen your understanding.

Connect interrelated facts through storytelling

I have a coworker who uses a special brand of synthesis to guide every business decision he makes: storytelling. In every business, there is a story of opportunity. In every memo, a story to explain the case for action. The strategy for our product comes down to the arc of its story to our customers. Even presentations, like well-crafted movies, build to a climax before unveiling a satisfying conclusion. His ability to stitch together seemingly unrelated threads into a tapestry makes him exceptional at detecting opportunities and also at identifying cleverly disguised gaps—he makes connections that go unnoticed by others. And it's this skill that makes him a great leader.

I use storytelling more often as a reflective tool rather than a predictive one. Summarizing my team's accomplishments in a story is more motivating than just showing facts and figures because it humanizes the effort into a narrative that everyone can understand.

Storytelling ultimately helps you clearly understand how events are interrelated by cause-and-effect relationships. When things go wrong, you will understand better how to prevent them from recurring if you recount them in a story. When things go right, you can use storytelling to better understand the drivers of your success.

EXAMPLE 1:

- **Fact 1:** The chicken was overcooked.
- **Fact 2:** I boiled it for 40 minutes.
- **Fact 3:** I cooked it on high heat.
- **You (Synthesis):** It sounds like the chicken was overcooked because you boiled it for too long and at too high a temperature. Is that correct?

EXAMPLE 2:

- **Facts:** Jack and Jill went up the hill to fetch a pail of water. Jack fell down and broke his crown, and Jill came tumbling after.
- **You (Synthesis):** It sounds like they never got the pail of water. Was that left at the top of the hill? Why did they need the water? Did they get any cuts or scratches from the fall that need Band-Aids?

EXAMPLE 3:

- **Head of Sales:** "Sales are at an all-time high!"
- **Head of Ops:** "Contracts signed are at an all-time low."

- **(Synthesis) CEO:** "It sounds like we have well-qualified prospects but the contracts are not completed yet. Is that correct or is there another reason why contracts and sales are not consistent?"

You may have different questions. You may draw different conclusions. The point is not to get it right the first time, but to use your conclusions as mechanism for drawing out more information. Only by synthesizing the full narrative of the story will you be able to uncover the truth.

Inference	**Sequencing**	**Storytelling**
For deeper understanding	*For identifying gaps in a process or plan*	*For understanding cause-and-effect relationships*
Merge multiple pieces of information together to draw conclusions.	List the information in order and look for missing steps.	Tell a story with the information and look for inconsistencies.

Three ways to synthesize information.

HOW TO SYNTHESIZE INFORMATION

Actively listen during conversations.
- Participate in conversations by asking questions and absorbing answers.

Summarize what you heard in your own words.
- Summarize in your own words, or ask someone to summarize for you. Doing so will force you to make sure you understand what was being said in a way that you can accurately communicate to others.
- Accurately represent the summary as it was stated. Do not embellish or add your opinion at this stage.

Merge multiple pieces of information together, then draw conclusions.
- Infer information: Extend the information with your own knowledge or assumptions to draw conclusions.
- Sequence information: Put all of the information in sequential order or plot it against a timeline. Look for missing steps or handoffs.
- Tell a story: Create a narrative that explains what happened. Extract lessons by looking at cause and effect.

Share your synthesis to confirm your extrapolations are correct.
- Share the conclusions you draw after synthesizing the information.
- Allow people to correct you. Then synthesize the information again until you are able to draw conclusions correctly.
- Capture the information you synthesized and share it out in writing to crystallize your learning.

PART II

How to Lay a Solid Foundation
for Your Project

CHAPTER 6

Create Alignment—It's the Best Way to Motivate Your Team

I was an impassioned violinist as a child. My big sister started playing violin in the fourth grade when she was offered the opportunity in elementary school, and I followed suit as soon as I was old enough to do the same. I played violin for five years after that and enjoyed every moment of it. As a result, I have genuine reverence for orchestral music. Bach's Brandenburg concertos never fail to fascinate me with their symmetry of rhythms. When I hear them, I vividly recall playing first violin for *Brandenburg Concerto No. 3* and feeling a surge of power when each stroke of my bow merged with the bows of my fellow violinists.

That love of classical music has also bloomed into fan-hood for movie-musicals such as *La La Land* and *The Greatest Showman*, which have been added to my playlist. When I listen to the music, I imagine a masterful conductor personifying the score, with her arms and fingers dancing gracefully to keep each note in its place, each bow moving in the right direction, each dramatic pause and reentry of the chorus happening at exactly the correct moment, in unison, to create that perfect song. (You can sometimes even catch me taking a walk, listening to the soundtracks, and waving my arms like a lunatic while I'm pretending to be the maestro.)

The harmony you hear when an orchestra performs synchronously together is, to me, a fitting example of perfect alignment. When projects are well aligned, everyone on the team knows the goal (the song to play), understands their part (the notes they need to play), and everything is timed perfectly according to the schedule. On the other hand, misaligned projects are fraught with notes that are out of tune, people who miss their cues, and people who are playing to entirely the wrong beat. As a project leader, it's your job to be the conductor who guides your team to find perfect harmony.

As soon as I'm assigned to a project, I begin aligning my team. Alignment starts with a strong relationship with your project sponsor. When I have a strong relationship with the people holding authoritative power on my project, their power implicitly extends to me when I am executing their will. This increases my influence to get things done, especially if I have no explicit authority over the team.

After a relationship with my sponsor is established, I work with the project leads to create clear goals. Those goals give me a target I can use to focus the efforts of every person on the team for the remainder of the project.

Build trust and open communication with your sponsor

In the fascinating book *The Gatekeepers: How the White House Chiefs of Staff Define Every Presidency*, author Chris Whipple recounts a pivotal conversation between President Jimmy Carter and his trusted advisor Jack Watson. Carter explains his reason for asking Watson to accept the role as his chief of staff: "You know my mind. You have a sense for my goals and I trust you implicitly to do this in the right spirit and in the right way." That type of trust is what makes the White House chief of staff the second most powerful person in the United States, next to the president.

The relationship that President Carter had with Watson is exactly the type of relationship I strive to cultivate with my project sponsors. Building infallible trust by executing faithfully on behalf of your sponsor allows you to wield her power in order to get things done. In the same way the White House chief of staff is able to tap into the power extended to them by the president, alignment with your sponsor will extend that person's power to you. That authority can also be used to force compliance even when a team member is resistant (as I'll share in chapter 12). And while using force is less desirable for my taste and not always necessary, I admit it is a handy tool that I can use to increase the urgency around tasks when I need them done quickly.

To create that trusting relationship, the first and most obvious task you need to do is to find your project sponsor. Early in my career, I never thought to even ask the question, "Who is the sponsor for this project?" With more experience, I learned that having a strong relationship with my sponsor gives me a lot of referential influence with my team. In addition, that relationship also allows me to solve situations that can only be resolved with formal authority. I realized my connection with the project sponsor was the one that would empower me most in my role.

If you are working on a project and you don't know your sponsor, don't be ashamed to ask. The easiest way to find the sponsor is to look for the person who holds the "keys to the cash," so to speak. Who is the person who funded your initiative? Who has the ability to pull the plug on it? That person is your sponsor. At most companies, there is always a designated executive for every project who is accountable for the overall execution. In a wedding, the sponsor may be the father of the bride, whoever is footing the bill. For my recent home remodeling project, the sponsor was me. I had veto power for any design choice made by our architect because I could refuse to pay for it.

Once you have identified your sponsor, you will want to tap into your newly cultivated skill to ask your effective questions. Well-formed questions build trust, and the most important question that you can ask to build trust with your sponsor is this one: "Why is this project important?" Use this question to start a robust conversation that will help you fully understand the underlying reasons for a project's importance, and its importance relative to other initiatives.

After your initial conversation, listen intently when your sponsor answers questions that arise in subsequent meetings for your project. Almost every sentence your sponsor speaks to address questions from others will provide you additional refinements to help you better understand what is important versus what is not. Listen carefully, synthesize what you heard, and ask clarifying questions when you are unsure if you can accurately communicate the reasoning to others. Understanding your sponsor's intention is paramount. That intention will become the key ingredient for synthesizing information on your project in the future; it will empower you to make the right in-the-moment judgment calls for your team even when the sponsor is not present.

Building trust and understanding intention takes time. Therefore, it's essential that you create a continuous, open line of communication with your sponsor for the course of your project. Your sponsor should have full transparency to what you do daily to support the project, and you should have direct access to your sponsor to make timely decisions when the choice is not obvious to you.

How you establish the open line of communication does not matter and should be chosen based on what is most convenient for your sponsor. One of my previous sponsors favored a "management by walking around" technique. He would take a stroll a couple of times a day and stop by my desk when he knew he would likely find me. We'd sync up for fifteen minutes to cover any big updates or new risks. (He also enjoyed the candy bowl I kept at my desk.)

Another sponsor sat next to me, so I never had to find her to have a conversation. We just chatted when the urge hit us. Yet another traveled often and had a packed meeting schedule. To stay in sync with him, I created a diary that I updated intraday in a digest format. He committed to reviewing the diary at minimum daily and would respond inline to any urgent questions. As a result, I always knew that questions would never sit more than a day. That timeliness allowed me to run the project with his guidance efficiently even when he wasn't physically present.

Set goals that are unambiguous to all team members

Once your relationship with your sponsor has been established and you understand the "why" behind the project, the next step is to work with the sponsor to create unambiguous goals. Ask your sponsor, "How will we know when this project is successful?" When you hear the first answer, ask follow-up questions until you fully understand the "what" and "when" in a way that you can explain it, and in a way that means the exact same thing to every person on the team, regardless of role.

A couple of years ago, I was working on a project for which the sponsor had set an elegant goal to "Launch 30 clients in 30 days." It had a nice ring to it and sounded clear at first blush. However, when I started to think about how I steer folks toward the goal, I realized I was confused by it. A litany of questions came rushing out of me.

- "When did the clock start? Do the thirty days include all days or just weekdays?" Since I just was assigned to the project, and it was already in flight, I had no idea which date we were targeting.
- "What does it mean to launch?" There were three teams involved—the sales team needed to sign contracts, the development team needed to deploy code to production for the feature, and our operations team needed to configure the client in order for them to be fully live. I realized quickly that each team thought the word *launch* meant something different, and I wanted to be certain that everyone was aimed at the same target.

- "Are we adding clients or just trying to get to a total of thirty?" We had eight clients live already, were we targeting an additional twenty-two or thirty more?
- "Are we targeting any type of client or just one client?" Did it matter where the clients were located? Was there a specific type of client we wanted?

Unambiguous goals are measurable, have a defined scope, timing, and mean the same thing to everyone. After an in-depth discussion, I had a stronger grasp of the intention and then proposed a revision bearing the attributes of unambiguous goals in mind. With that stronger sense of clarity, I broadcast the refined goal to our team to dispel possible misconceptions.

Before	Revised for clarity
Launch 30 clients in 30 days	Go live to all of our consumer website users with X feature with an additional 30 clients in the LA region by October 1, XXXX

One of the most compelling stories I've heard that illustrates the importance of setting an unambiguous goal is one that a Hawaiian friend of mine likes to tell about a series of tunnels that were hand-dug by Chinese laborers near the sugar cane fields on the island of Kauai in the early 1800s. My friend, who has lived on the island his whole life, marvels at this feat. To finish long tunnels faster, laborers were instructed to dig tunnels in from the opposite sides of large mountains. At a time when technology was limited, it is fascinating that they were able to meet in the middle to create one continuous tunnel. Had there been a miscalculation in either direction, it could have resulted in a massive literal disconnect.

These Chinese laborers didn't complete the feat alone though. They had help from people like Clarence S. Koike, whose job it was to guide them. According to the history book *The Seven Dawns of the*

Aumakua, "[Clarence's] first job assignment at Kekaha was to act as a navigator in tunnel construction in the Kokee area, where many aqueducts or ditches were under construction to bring water to the cane fields on the lower ridges above Mana, Kekaha, and Waimea. A number of these tunnels were dug simultaneously from both ends to meet hundreds of feet underground. It was Clarence's job to enter the tunnels and take compass readings to ensure that both ends were heading in the proper direction for joining."

When all of the moving parts must come together to achieve success, a miscalculation in your target can result in a fairly large miss at the point of delivery. You can be the Clarence who keeps your team focused and headed in the right direction by starting with a clear goal, and then using it to guide them.

Establish partnerships with your team leads

Next to your sponsor, the most critical relationships to form will be those with the leads of your functional teams. For example, if you are managing a software development project, you may need to work with a product lead, a technical lead, and a quality assurance lead. If you are working on a home construction project, the leads may be the construction manager and your architect. Your team leads are the people who will be managing the work queue for anyone who is doing hands-on work for your project. Take the time to meet with them individually and establish a connection with them.

Share the unambiguous goal that you created with your team leads to make sure they understand its meaning and that it is truly unambiguous. The best test of a goal is to review it with multiple team members, in particular from cross-functional teams, and then have them tell you what the goal means to them. Ask them if there is anything about the goal that seems ambiguous to them and then work to refine the phrasing until it is well understood and self-explanatory. This step will also help garner buy-in from your leads for your initiative.

After clarifying the goals, the most important task will be to make sure you are establishing a partnership with your leads. Discuss the responsibilities you will each hold, questions or concerns that are on their minds, and discuss ways you can work together to mitigate them. Asking questions and capturing what you hear from these conversations will help you build trust and rapport. In addition, having these frank conversations up front will set a precedent for strong communication among you and your leads as the project progresses. Don't forget to suggest areas where you can help so that they can see the immediate value you will bring to the team.

Finally, work with your team leads to confirm you have all the right people with the skills needed to complete your project. As partners in crime, your team leads can help you make sure you are identifying any missing skills on the team so that you can push to get the appropriate people assigned to help. If you need additional team members, then work with your sponsor to assign individuals to fill those gaps before you kick off your project.

Conduct a kickoff meeting to mark the start of your project

Once you have a clear goal and commitment from your team leads, then you will want to broadcast that goal to the team at large. A kickoff is a fairly simple but critical step in the team-forming phase because it's the first time you will officially get the full team together.

The objective of the kickoff is to ensure everyone on the project has the same basis of understanding before you start work and feels fully ready to get started. Use a kickoff meeting to officially mark the start of the project. Collect all the information you have to date on the project and invite all team members to a meeting. Ask the sponsor to share why the project is important so that your team can hear the "why" behind their work. Review the goals, the team assignments and areas of responsibility. Allot time for questions and then close with next steps so that people in the meeting are ready to be mobilized as soon as your kickoff ends.

Topics to cover in a kickoff meeting.

Connect daily work to a purpose

If you have never watched Derek Sivers's TED talk, *How to Start a Movement*, I highly recommend it. It is only 2 minutes and 54 seconds but packs a punch of a message, all while entertaining you with the silliness of a group of free spirits dancing on the grass. I love the line, "The first follower transforms a lone nut into a leader. If the leader is the flint, the first follower is the spark that makes the fire."

While my project sponsors may not want to proclaim they are the "lone nut" of the project, I'd happily declare myself the first follower. When I'm leading projects, my most important responsibility is to align my team by showing others how to follow.

Armed with deputized power from your sponsor and the benefit of clear goals, leading by example is easy. Just repeat the goal, often and through every communication medium. Why all the duplication?

I've learned through experience that people learn in a number of different ways—some through reading, some through listening, some only when those are combined, or they are acting on something. The repetition guarantees I'm leaving no gap in which anyone can miss it. The goal needs to permeate every layer of the team so that there is no lack of clarity about where we are headed together.

Next, I reinforce the importance of every role and every task by continually connecting back to the goal. When a developer is working on a story, I tell them why the story is important. When the impact of the feature we launched is known, I tell them how that same story made a difference in our overall goals. When a designer is thinking through the design of a new user interface, I tell them again why the design is important in reaching the goal. When the release team is working late at night on a deployment, I tell them how grateful we are that they will help us get these features to production because of the progress it will allow us to make toward our goal.

I am continually connecting each task to the purpose and acknowledging the importance of the work being done. When people understand how their work matters, they feel more highly motivated because they know their work is contributing to a greater vision.

In *The Power of Moments*, authors Chip Heath and Dan Heath help us understand why aligning the team matters. They said, "But for groups, defining moments arise when we create shared meaning—highlighting the mission that binds us together and supersedes our differences. We are made to feel united." Propagating a shared sense of meaning is how you conduct your own orchestra to drive team harmony.

HOW TO CREATE ALIGNMENT

Align with your executive sponsor.
- Find your sponsor by asking who has the ability to defund the project.
- Build trust by asking questions, including, "Why is this project important?"
- Establish an ongoing, open line of communication.

Create unambiguous goals.
- A clear goal means the same thing to everyone who reads it.
- Work with your sponsor to refine your goal to cover the "what" and "when" and broadcast that goal to everyone on your team.

Conduct a kickoff meeting.
- Gather everyone on your project into a meeting and review the goals, responsibility, and logistics so that everyone on the project has the same basis of understanding.

Connect daily work to a purpose.
- Repeat the goal often, and through all communication mediums.
- Explain why each role and task matters, and how it is contributing to shared goals daily.

◆ ◆◆

CHAPTER 7

Does Every Project Need a Plan? Nope, Planning Is Optional

You may be surprised to learn that when I originally outlined this book, I didn't include a chapter on planning. Do I plan? Of course I do. I've even been accused of loving plans. Do I think a project leader needs to be able to whip up a solid plan at a moment's notice? Yes, absolutely. But do I think that every project needs a plan? Nope, plans are optional.

Every project needs a clear goal and an engaged and accountable team that knows what needs to be done to achieve that goal. But not every project needs a formal, written project plan.

The term *project plan* evokes a familiar (and sometimes unfavorable) image for most—a detailed list in Microsoft Project with a bunch of line items, dates, names, and a pretty Gantt chart. It's the stuff that a lot of project management books and newly certified project managers swear by. However, on the majority of projects I've led, that type of plan has never been necessary. The last time I put together a Gantt chart was over ten years ago, and I did it because I was working on a project for a client who liked Gantt charts. It made them feel like the project was under control.

But before that, I had successfully launched projects for several clients without one. And since then, I've delivered projects for the last ten years without one. Shockingly, none of the projects I've led without detailed project plans have failed. On the contrary, they have flourished.

Many new project managers will often start with a default stance that their job is to create a detailed plan and maintain it. They chase their team to create lists, lists of lists, and more detailed lists of lists. They spend their days pestering the team for updates so that they can update their detailed lists. And before you know it, their days are primarily consumed by playing catch-up and updating the plan instead of helping the team get things done. It's a recipe for failure.

Planning is not useful to your team when it's only a reflection of the past. It's most useful when it helps you get things done in the future.

Project planning is *not* the same as project leading. And your job is to lead the project.

For me, effectively leading a project means that everything I'm doing is boosting team productivity. Therefore, the main criterion I use to decide whether I should create a plan is the answer to this question: "Will planning help my team?" If so, then I plan. If my team is confused about what to do, I create a plan. If my team tells me they need a plan, I create a plan. I plan the minimum amount that will be helpful and useful to make sure the team knows what they need to do. No more, no less.

We now live in a culture where any company that is looking to move faster and with less waste subscribes to Agile methodologies—build incrementally, fail fast. Teams have defined workflows they use to get work done every day, and they are highly productive when they use processes they already have to churn out work. Your team will benefit when you plan to complement their current workflows, when you are boosting their productivity instead of slowing them down to check off items on your list.

When you adjust your view of the world to be team centric, you will see that plans are most helpful when they are used sparingly and intentionally to solve a particular problem for your team. The right plan motivates your team, guides them in the right direction, and helps them in a crunch. That's how I use planning, and I believe it is also one of the reasons my teams do well.

Having said all that, when your team needs a plan, you should have the skill to craft one quickly. And that's why I ultimately added this chapter to the book—so that you can choose the planning method that best suits your team and have the confidence to do it well. The next sections will focus on a variety of planning methods that you can use depending on your teams' needs.

Create mini-goals using milestones

The most effective type of plan is one that is simple but provides enough guidance so that your team knows what they need to do. The lightest-weight plan contains two components: (1) clear goals and (2) milestones. Since I've already discussed how you set unambiguous goals to create alignment, I'll focus here on how to create milestones.

A milestone is just a mini-goal. Therefore, if you have a very short project (two weeks or shorter), milestones may not be needed. The main reason to create milestones is to make your big, overarching goals feel more achievable. While big goals can be inspiring, they can also be demoralizing if they feel too far out of reach. Using milestones to break big goals into smaller steps can alleviate anxiety and help your team envision a path to success. That should be your primary guide to determining whether or not you feel milestones are needed.

Like a clear, unambiguous goal, well-defined milestones will have a "what" that means the same thing to everyone on the project as well as a "when." The series of milestones for your project will then build toward your overarching goal. As your project progresses, these milestones will also help you understand if your project is on the right trajectory to succeed or if you need to recalibrate.

I've used three different methods to define milestones: (1) logical chunks of work, (2) sub-metrics, and (3) meaningful accomplishments. The first, and probably the most popular, way to set milestones is to break up your project into logical chunks of work. This method is similar to what you might do if you are defining a traditional project plan and is most applicable when you are leading a project that has a well-defined end state.

As an example, if a client wants you to build a website in six months, you might deliver one page at a time. If you are renovating your home, you might pay your contractor once the crew has broken ground, built the frame, completed interior build-out, and then added the finishings. If you are planning a wedding, then the chunks of work are fairly logical too: book your venue, get a wedding dress, send out invites, and then have the actual wedding. When you define milestones this way, they should be self-explanatory. They should be chunks of work that are big enough to show reasonable progress. And they should be unlikely to change over time.

The second method is simple as well because it's metric based. In the last chapter I provided an example goal where we were aiming to launch thirty clients in thirty days. A logical interim milestone for that project would have been fifteen clients in two weeks, or even seven per week. Aiming high for weekly milestones provides a little cushion to meeting the overall goal. For writing this book, I could have broken down the milestones into chapters or into word count. I ended up choosing word count because the chapters could vary in size, and I wanted a reliable way to understand how I was tracking toward creating a book with enough content that I could publish it.

Metric-based goals and milestones work best when the end state of a project is unknown but you have a clear timeline. They allow you to change tactics midstream without compromising the overarching goals you've set for your team. This makes them durable over the course of your project.

In my more recent product development projects, we use a hybrid of these two tactics for defining milestones. For the initial phase of the project, when we're just trying to build a minimally viable product (MVP), the milestones are defined as logical chunks of work based on the features we aim to build. Then, once the MVP is launched, we switch to a metric-based approach. That's also when we start to embrace an iterative product development cycle where we develop theories to test, launch them, and then measure their impact. At that point, we are looking for customer adoption as a measure of success so metrics that help us understand engagement are better suited for helping us understand if we are on the right trajectory to our goals.

In *The Power of Moments*, authors Chip Heath and Dan Heath offer yet a third method for defining milestones, with a clever twist that can also boost motivation. "A wise leader can look for milestones en route to a larger goal . . . ask yourself: What's inherently motivating? What would be worth celebrating that might only take a few weeks or months of work? What's a hidden accomplishment that is worth surfacing and celebrating?"

Their advice is to capitalize on the fact that people feel good when they reach goals by breaking goals into small, personal, meaningful goals that can be achieved on the path to that larger goal. Doing so creates more opportunities for celebration, thus multiplying the positive effect on the path to achievement.

As an example, my mom wears both an Apple watch and a Fitbit (one on each wrist). Both wearables use this method of milestone setting to define miniature, personal goals for her. As a retiree, my mom uses these devices to motivate her to keep moving. She looks forward to achieving her walking, breathing, and exercise goals each day. Nothing makes her prouder than receiving the news that she has completed all of her health rings for the day—she even sends happy emojis to my sister and me via text to celebrate when she achieves them. These milestones create daily positive feelings for her as she makes progress on her path to her long-term health.

To apply this method to milestone setting, you would identify milestones that are more personal in nature rather than metric-based. For example, if you are aiming to increase the quality of customer service, you may want to celebrate when your first five-star review is received. Once that is achieved, you might then celebrate once you have finished one full week without any major customer complaints.

On the other hand, if your goal is to become a successful project leader, you might reward yourself the first time you are complimented on your meeting notes. You might applaud yourself when you have five successive meetings that end on time. You might cheer quietly when you hear team members from two different functional teams explain the goal of your project with identical precision.

Regardless of how you define the milestones, you should involve your sponsor and the most senior members of your project team. You want to validate that the milestones are well understood and

Logical Chunks of Work	**Metric-Based Targets**	**Meaningful Milestones**
For projects with a defined end state & features list	*For projects with goals that are metric based*	*For operational or performance-based projects*

Define your milestone by logical chunks of work. They should be almost self-explanatory and easy to understand by everyone.	Take the metric for your overarching goal and split it into increments. Make the increments more aggressive to provide a cushion.	Choose inherently motivating events, such as high customer ratings, that are also accurate markers of progress toward the goal.

Methods for defining milestones.

that others have fully bought into your plan. The milestones should be clear and aggressive, but feel achievable so that they can serve as both a motivating and anchoring force for the day-to-day execution of the project.

Set clear priorities so teams know what's important

The next level of fidelity for a plan is to set clear priorities based on the milestones and goals. The priorities help the teams understand what to do first. After that, you just lean on their current workflows and watch for progress of the work being done.

A few years ago, I was pulled into a meeting to discuss a project we were about to kick off that would require changes across the entire website. We had six teams working on website products at that time, and each one would need to do some work. The problem was that all of these teams had their own projects that were already in flight, and this project was a curve ball. Since the project had a high level of urgency, we were faced with the drawback of disrupting all their work and also tanking morale.

There was a feeling that we would need a heavy-handed approach to managing this project, that it would likely require a detailed plan so that the teams would be well coordinated and the goals would be met under a tight timeline. But I suggested a different approach. Why not educate the teams on what needed to be done, give them a time-line, and then trust them to do it? All the teams had product owners who could flesh out requirements for that work, developers who were talented enough to get the work done quickly, and defined workflows for delivering work. Why not take advantage of the processes that were already in place and give the teams the autonomy to handle it their way?

We ended up creating a list of all the pages that needed to be touched and sorting them in priority order. Then we assigned groups of pages to individual teams. We provided instructions for the changes needed for each page and guidelines for decisions to be made at the discretion of the team. We gave them a deadline to get all the work done. And then we created a dashboard in JIRA, a task tracking software, to track the statuses of the changes as they were completed.

To our delight, the approach worked. Teams took accountability for their assignments and weaved them into their current roadmaps. It allowed them to continue in-flight work without feeling as if we were derailing efforts. It gave them a sense of control and autonomy to use their current workflows to get tasks done in the most efficient manner for their team. All the high-priority items were tackled. All the teams completed their changes swiftly, and most were done ahead of the deadline.

I've recently started referring to this paradigm for leading projects as the CALM method, where CALM stands for "Closely Aligned, Loosely Managed." What's clever about the name is that it also reflects the state of mind of the project leader. When you have confidence that your team is aligned with the right priorities and you trust them to get things done, it also makes you a much calmer leader.

For my most recent project, we also used the CALM method for planning. We had an overarching goal for the year. We chopped the target into monthly milestones and worked toward the goal iteratively, doing minimal planning at the top of every month.

Each month, we recalibrated based on our current progress and shared the next milestone with the team. We worked together with our sponsor to create a prioritized list of features we wanted to build to hit the target. Finally, with the priorities clear, our development team used a Kanban workflow (which is essentially the software development equivalent of a manufacturer's just-in-time paradigm) to push features out the door one by one. Throughout the development cycle, we reinforced priorities so that most important features always made it to production first. By the end of the year, we hit our target almost on the nose (overachieving just slightly).

The CALM method works best when you have teams that are already accountable and have their own methods for shipping work. In distributed work environments or environments of large conglomerate teams, CALM also works particularly well because it allows each of the sub-teams to use the processes that work best for them to achieve the desired outcomes. To use CALM, set goals and milestones, and then clear priorities. Continually anchor the team on what's most important. Ask the teams to take responsibility for reporting their own progress. Then get out of the way and let the experts do their work.

Create roadmaps to build team confidence

Roadmaps are best used when you have a larger goal over a series of months and your project has a relatively predefined end state. A *roadmap* is essentially a high-level representation of tasks that are organized in parallel work streams and sequenced over time. A roadmap is useful to help your team

- Understand parallel streams of work,
- Gain a better sense for how you might sequence the work,
- Identify dependencies on other teams well ahead of the need, and
- Build enough confidence to start work.

When I create a roadmap, I typically use Post-it notes. I grab my team and pull them into a room with a big, empty wall. I draw or tape lines on the wall to create a grid that reflects the roadmap I want to create, then fill in each box using Post-it notes for each item that needs to be completed. The beauty of this method is that it is easy to do and also extremely collaborative. Everyone on my team can write tasks on individual Post-it notes. I can help place the notes, move them around, or adjust as needed to assemble the roadmap right in front of my team. No fancy tool or skills necessary.

Once the roadmap is finished, I then take photos of the wall so that we have a digital copy of it. After the meeting, I migrate the roadmap to a digital format, such as a spreadsheet, an electronic document, or the corresponding project management tool that my team uses for ongoing updates.

An alternative is to use a spreadsheet from the beginning to collaborate electronically, but I find that Post-its are far more collaborative if people are available in person. There may be other online tools you can use, but I've never found a need for anything more sophisticated than Post-it notes or spreadsheets, and using tools that people already know how to use is always best.

The simplest and least prescriptive roadmap is called a *fuzzy roadmap*. Fuzzy roadmaps are best when you want to get a little more granularity than general priorities provide but don't feel the need to box the team into specific dates. This method is compatible with a Kanban workflow and essentially categorizes work into fuzzy timeframes of now, soon, and later. Now should be used for anything you want to start work on immediately. Soon identifies work that should be queued up next. Later is almost like a backlog—it captures items that you want to tackle eventually but are not as urgent and therefore will be done last.

A *work stream* is a group of related work that should be done serially. For example, in a wedding you may define a work stream as all the activities related to budgeting. First you would need to set your budget, then create a savings plan, or ask for additional contributions from your parents. An *epic* is a collection of smaller items that are related to one another. For example, the epic of setting your budget may entail quite a few underlying tasks such as doing research on wedding, venue and invitation costs, then looking at your monthly spending levels to determine actions you can take to save money.

Work streams	Now	Soon	Later
Work stream 1	Epic 1	Epic 4	Epic 5
Work stream 2	Epic 2	Epic 6	Epic 6
Work stream 3	Epic 3	Epic 7	Epic 7

Fuzzy roadmap format.

Work streams	Now	Soon	Later
Wedding Funding	—Set a budget —Start saving money		
Wedding Dress	—Try on dresses	—Order dress	—Get alterations
Wedding Event	—Research wedding locations	—Book wedding location & date	—Food and decorations
Invite Guests	—Ask parents for guest list	—Consolidate guest list —Order invitations —Get a room block	—Send invitations
Honeymoon	—Research honeymoon locations	—Book honeymoon —Get passports	—Pack for honeymoon

Example: Wedding plan fuzzy roadmap.

Work streams	Now	Soon	Later
Website Infrastructure	—Build out development & testing environment	—Build out production environment	—Create monitoring for production environment & escalation handling procedures
Platform Development	—Procedure required data to drive website logic and display	—Build out back-end services to make required data available	—Optimize services to website performance standards
Front End Design	—Design for high priority pages	—Design for medium priority pages	—Design for low priority pages
Front End Development		—Build out front-end pages with mock data	—Build out front-end pages with real data
Cutover Plan		—Discuss cutover timing and risks, and contingencies	—Flush out cutover plan details
Training		—Get input from stakeholders	—Build out training materials and schedule training

Example: Website build-out fuzzy roadmap.

A more detailed version of a roadmap is one that is time based. A *time-based roadmap* is helpful when your goal has a hard target date and you want to understand if the desired scope is achievable by the deadline. It can also be helpful if you need to provide stakeholders a better estimate for when features might be completed. A time-based roadmap is identical to a fuzzy one, except the columns will reflect a unit of time (weeks, sprints, or months) until the project needs to be completed.

Work streams	Month 1	Month 2	Month 3	Month 4	Month 5
Work stream 1	Epic 1	Epic 4	Epic 5	Epic 8	Epic 10
Work stream 2	Epic 2	Epic 6	Epic 6	Epic 9	Epic 11
Work stream 3	Epic 3	Epic 7	Epic 7	Epic 7	Epic 12

Time-based roadmap format.

Work streams	Month 1	Month 2	Month 3	Month 4	Month 5
Wedding Budget	Start saving	Set a budget		Finish saving	
Wedding Dress	Research dresses	Order a dress		Find a tailor	Get alterations
Wedding Event	Research venues	Book a venue	Research vendors for food & decorations	Book & pay vendor deposits	
Invite Guests	Ask parents for guest list	Get a room block	Order invitations	Consolidated guest list & mail invitations	Tally RSVPs & create seat plan
Honeymoon		Research locations	Order passports	Book honeymoon	Pack for honeymoon

Example: Wedding plan time-based roadmap.

Similar to milestones, building a roadmap is most useful when you create it with your project sponsor and the leads from your project team. You need their expertise to complete it and assurance that what you produce will be helpful to them.

HOW TO CREATE A ROADMAP

Create a grid for your roadmap.

- For a fuzzy roadmap, use *now, soon,* and *later* across the top.
- For a time-based roadmap, use *weeks, sprints,* or *months* across the top.
- Add resources or parallel streams of work in the left-hand column.

Write out "epic" level units of work.

- In the world of Agile development, an epic is a collection of items that are related to one another and serve to deliver specific customer value. It's usually something that can and should be broken into smaller pieces for delivery.

Plot and sequence the topics.

- Collaborate with your team to plot out the work in a logical sequence choosing the appropriate timeframe. *Now* would be used for anything you want to start work on immediately. *Soon* identifies work that should be queued up next. *Later* is almost like a backlog—it captures items that you want to tackle eventually but are not as urgent and therefore will be done last.

Consider dependencies.

- As you plot your epics, take into consideration streams of work that can be done in parallel and possible dependencies.

Create detailed task lists sparingly and intentionally

The final type of plan is the most granular one and is most closely related to a traditional project plan: a detailed task list. Task lists are best used sparingly and intentionally. To construct a task list, simply gather everyone who has a part to play, state the goal, ask them what needs to be done, and then synthesize the information by sequencing it.

I don't recommend task lists for creating a comprehensive plan for any large project because they tend to get outdated quickly. As an example, my husband, who is now the CTO at a small start-up, recently recounted a story to me about the one and only time he created a detailed task list and a Gantt chart. After spending a week working with his project manager to make sure it was complete, he shared the project plan with his project sponsor only to be told that he needed to cut the scope and timeline in half. "It was totally useless," he recalls.

To prevent that type of energy waste, I recommend using detailed task lists only when you truly need them. The scenario when they are most useful is when you have a tight timeline and tasks that need to be closely coordinated across multiple teams or people who don't usually work together. For example, a big or complicated feature release or code deployment might warrant tighter control. In this type of scenario, spend a meeting or two assembling the task list quickly. Use it for the few days it is needed and then retire it as soon as all the tasks are completed.

Planning to boost team productivity requires agility on the part of the project leader to know what type of plan will best fit the needs of the team. Use these methods deliberately to create the least overhead for yourself, spend less time chasing updates, and save more time to do work that creates the highest benefit for your team.

Task	Who	Priority	Status	Estimated Effort	Due Day	Due Time	Additional Notes
Website Feature Deployment							
Back-end services to provide data for the page	Aryan	MUST DO	DONE	2 Hours			
Apply database updates to integration environment	Lee	MUST DO	DONE	2 Hours	Tues 7/24/2021	12:00 PM	
Complete all configuration updates	Lee	MUST DO	DONE	2 Hours	Tues 7/24/2021	12:00 PM	
Front-end development	Kim	MUST DO	DONE	1 Hour	Tues 7/24/2021	2:00 PM	
Deploy to integration environment	Aryan	MUST DO	TO DO	1 Hour	Tues 7/24/2021	3:00 PM	
QA Testing / Smoke Test	Mina	MUST DO	TO DO	1 Hour	Tues 7/24/2021	4:00 PM	We have been having issues with 500 errors coming from the hosts and we want to watch this to confirm all is good.
Run Automated Regression Tests	Mina	MUST DO	TO DO	30 Minutes	Tues 7/24/2021	4:30 PM	
Product QA	Anh	MUST DO	TO DO	30 Minutes	Tues 7/24/2021	5:00 PM	
Sign-off to deploy to prod	Anh	MUST DO	TO DO	1 Hour	Tues 7/24/2021	5:30 PM	
Deploy to Staging Environment	Aryan	MUST DO	TO DO	1 Hour	Tues 7/24/2021	6:00 PM	
Complete all database & configuration updates in staging	Lee	MUST DO	TO DO	1 Hour	Tues 7/24/2021	6:30 PM	
Smoke test in staging	Mina	MUST DO	TO DO	1 Hour	Tues 7/24/2021	7:00 PM	
Complete all database & configuration updates in prod	Lee	MUST DO	TO DO	1 Hour	Tues 7/24/2021	7:30 PM	
Deploy to prod	Aryan	MUST DO	TO DO	1 Hour	Tues 7/24/2021	8:00 PM	
Smoke Test in production	Mina	MUST DO	TO DO	1 Hour	Tues 7/24/2021	8:30 PM	

Example: Detailed task list for website deployment.

Goals + Milestones 	Best For: Longer running projects (multi-month) where the goal may be too big. Helps the team by: Breaking the goal into smaller, incremental milestones makes it feel more achievable.
Priorities (CALM Method) 	Best For: Teams that already have a well-defined and efficient workflow for getting work done. Helps the team by: Providing clear direction on the most important work to complete, while providing the teams autonomy to get it done their way.
Roadmaps 	Best For: Projects that have a defined end state and take place over a period of weeks or months. Helps the team by: Sanity checking scope, understanding sequencing of work, and identifying dependencies sooner rather than later.
Detailed Task Lists 	Best For: Shorter efforts that require tight coordination, in particular when the people don't work together frequently. Helps the team by: Providing clarity on the individual tasks to be done, the handoffs that need to take place, and providing a common view of statuses.

Layers of planning.

HOW TO CREATE A DETAILED TASK LIST

State and discuss the goal.
* Your team must understand what you are aiming to reach when the list is completed.

Identify all the tasks.
* Ask the team what needs to be done to achieve your goal, and write down all the tasks.

Assign accountability for each task.
* Ask: "Who can do this?" (or "Who has the skills to do this?")
* Ask: "When can it be done?" (or "When will you know when it can be done?")

Identify dependencies for each task.
* Ask: "Does anything need to happen before it can be done?" (or "Can this be done in parallel to other tasks?")
* If you want to get fancy, you can also record dependencies to make it a full-on Gantt chart. I find having a notes column to capture any dependencies is sufficient.

Synthesize your task list.
* Capture the tasks, owner, and a proposed due date.
* Put the tasks in order in a logical sequence considering dependencies.

Recap to confirm accuracy and completeness.
* Recap the list in order for items you've compiled.
* Ask if there are any holes to meeting the goal. Patch the holes until everyone agrees your task list looks correct to all participants.

CHAPTER 8

How to Safely Jump Out of a Plane (Tips for Preempting Risk)

I was looking out the window as the airplane climbed in altitude, watching as the buildings and cars became smaller and smaller and I couldn't spot the landing site anymore. The pilot announced, "We're getting close to 10,000 feet," and my heart just sank. I started to wonder why a perfectly sane adult would decide to jump out of a perfectly safe airplane.

I'd always considered myself risk averse. At the age of twenty-two, I had my own car insurance, health insurance, and even a retirement savings account. I wasn't the type to go skydiving. But my friend had convinced me to go, and I had signed all my rights away before I got on the plane. I was beyond the point of no return. Minutes later, I'd be hurtling toward the earth whether I liked it or not.

Despite all the adrenaline and doubt I had in the moment, jumping out of the plane was actually a fairly calculated risk. Prior to the plane ride, I had attended an eight-hour Accelerated Free Fall (AFF) training course for first-time skydivers who want to jump out of a plane solo—you learn the skills to skydive alone, without an instructor attached to your back, after they help you take the initial leap from the plane.

We talked about how skydivers spend three hours painstakingly packing their chutes using a technique that significantly increases the likelihood the chute will open correctly. We learned that there are two different cords to trigger your chute in case the first doesn't work. We talked about what to do if your chute didn't open fully and how to correct it midair. We learned how to fall in a way that minimized the number of broken bones in our bodies in a worst-case scenario.

When you start to learn more about all the safety measures of the sport, you realize that some of the people you view as the biggest risk takers are also the people who are the most risk averse. They go through great lengths to make sure that risks don't manifest, but they also learn the skills to know exactly what to do should risks arise. This is why extreme skiers will learn how to identify unstable skiing conditions, but also undergo avalanche training. Long distance swimmers will train in cold water to condition their bodies for prolonged exposure to cold temperatures, but also learn how to monitor for and treat symptoms of hypothermia.

You may not equate leading projects to an extreme sport, but there are parallels. All projects have risk. Project leaders are often brought onto a project to help reduce the risk and to meet an important deadline. Therefore, understanding how to best manage risk is important to the success of that role. Project leaders attack projects with a certain amount of bravery and the confidence that they can withstand any risk that presents itself, just as I prepared to jump out of that plane. They anticipate risk, prepare their teams for it, but then also have the know-how to adapt in a worst-case scenario. While other chapters in this book are aimed at giving you the skills to adapt when things don't go smoothly, this chapter is devoted to preempting risk before it occurs.

Every project is unique, but you can usually preempt common risks in the early phases. The first common risk is scope creep, which I will address in detail in chapter 11. In the coming sections, I'll address four additional common risks I've seen and provide some recommendations on how to handle each of them.

Prevent burnout by saving heroism for when it counts

On every aggressive project, you will risk burning out your team. According to the article "Job Burnout: How to Spot It and Take Action" by the Mayo Clinic staff, "Job burnout is a special type of work-related stress—a state of physical or emotional exhaustion that also involves a sense of reduced accomplishment and loss of personal identity." Burnout will happen if you push your team to work at elevated stress levels for long periods of time. Burnout will cause your projects to fail because people will either ask to leave your project, or their productivity will be decreased and you will miss your dates.

To prevent burnout, save heroism for times that truly matter. On big projects, you'll be under a lot of pressure to ask your team to sprint a marathon. It's just not humanly possible. There are few cases when I will advocate challenging your project sponsor, but this is one case where you should stand your ground every time. If a sponsor is asking me to push my team too hard, too early, and when the impact of that hard work is not meaningful, I will push back by proposing options that are more manageable or seek to cut the scope. To be clear, I have no objection to asking a team to work hard when it counts. Great teams are forged in times of adversity. However, acts of heroism must actually translate into important results. If they do not, you will lose your team when you need them most.

When you truly need your team to pull an act of heroism, then make every effort to ensure your team is happy and motivated while they are doing it. You have the ability to make this possible by explaining why they are being asked to go above and beyond the normal call of duty and supporting them while they are being stretched.

Mo Gawdat, former chief business officer for Google X, credits having accurate expectations as one key to being happy in life and work. In his book *Solve for Happy*, he says: "Unhappiness happens when your reality does not match your hopes and expectations ... which means that if you perceive the events as equal to or greater than your expectations, you're happy—or at least not unhappy. But here's the tricky bit: it's not the event that makes us unhappy; it's the way we think about it that does."

When you need your team to work hard, make it clear in your request exactly how much effort you need from them. Being direct with them up front prepares them mentally for the amount of work to come and avoids future disconnects in expectations.

Similar to what I discussed in chapter 6 for aligning your teams, you can also motivate your team by connecting their work to a purpose. Before they start work, they should understand why it's important. (Remember that people like to have reasons for what they do.) If they believe their work is important, it will improve the frame of mind under which they approach their work. After they become heroes, honor them with praise that is specific and connects their work to the impact it had on your project to reinforce the message. Keeping your team motivated by showing them that their hard work matters will, in turn, help prevent burnout.

Finally, don't forget to tend to your teams' needs if they are working overtime. Keep them well fed by offering to pay for meals and keeping a stock of favorite snacks. Make sure they are resting by granting time off after they sprint. These seem like small offerings, but they show that you care. And when you are asking your team to work hard for you, they will appreciate your extra effort to show support.

Use a premortem to identify blind spots

Blind spots are another major risk, in particular to large projects that have many stakeholders. I use the term *blind spot* to describe a body of work that was missed because no one on your project thought to do it. These can be difficult to identify, but not impossible. You can surface blind spots by crowdsourcing possible risks from your team using an exercise that is called a premortem.

Gary Klein, writing in the *Harvard Business Review*, provides this definition: "A premortem in a business setting comes at the beginning of a project rather than the end, so that the project can be improved rather than autopsied. Unlike a typical critiquing session, in which project team members are asked what might go wrong, the premortem operates on the assumption that the 'patient' has died, and so asks what did go wrong. The team members' task is to generate plausible reasons for the project's failure."

To perform a premortem, pull your project team into a meeting after you've initially kicked off the project and your team understands the goals. In the premortem, frame the exercise in the context of the future. Ask this: "Imagine we are now three months out from the launch of this project, and it has failed. What went wrong?" Then ask everyone on the team to write down possible causes for failure to share with the group.

Premortems can be used to extract concerns from your team members in a nonthreatening way. They can also help you win buy-in from skeptical team members. I recall the first time I held a premortem, one of the stakeholders who had been exhibiting signs of resistance during the project kickoff exclaimed, "This is so cathartic!" She was relieved to share all of her worries and get them off her chest. After the premortem, she was also more bought-in to the success of the project because she felt we had properly discussed all the possible risks. She was confident that we would be able to handle her concerns down the road.

Often, a premortem will help you successfully identify groups of people who may be affected by your project but were missed in the initial kickoff discussions. Usually they are people who work downstream from your product or may have a small role to play but weren't core to the meat of the project. For example, the team that has to publish a piece of content to support development, or the customer service team that has to update an FAQ for your customers. They are examples of classic blind spots that, left unidentified, can create delays down the line.

The result of an effective premortem is a successfully crowd-sourced and discussed list of possible risks that might derail your project. It's an unconventional way to get your team to surface concerns that they may have been afraid to vocalize. In addition, it can help you detect blind spots and open them up for discussion.

Once the brainstorming has ended, I recommend codifying the list of the causes of failure into a document and then assigning domain experts to the items that are perceived to be the highest risk. At this point, rather than creating detailed plans, trust the team to do their job. If they know the goals and take ownership over their respective areas of expertise, they will also do their best to mitigate those risks.

Reduce bottlenecks through redundancy

Bottlenecks occur on your project when there is too much work going into one team or person than can be handled in a timely fashion. For example, if all stories need to go through a QA (quality assurance) cycle, and you have four developers completing stories and one QA person, then the QA person will quickly become a bottleneck if they cannot keep up with the work for the four developers. As a result, stories will take longer to get through QA than expected, which will cause the overall productivity of the team to slow.

Bottlenecks are apt to happen when teams are overly specialized and also draw hard lines between responsibilities when they work. The best way to prevent bottlenecks is to create redundancy when you are choosing or training your team so that people are willing and able to pitch in as an alternate on roles that may not be their primary function. In chapter 10, I will talk about how project leaders can expedite handoffs by plugging gaps. When they are plugging gaps, the project leader is acting as a redundant layer for those tasks. Other team members can be trained or prepared to do the same. In product development teams, product owners and designers can help with QA testing. Back-end developers may be able to pitch in on front-end work. Developers can help to write stories and flush out acceptance criteria.

When you create redundancy in skill sets across your teams, and you set expectations that individuals on the team can and should support one another when work is not moving at an optimal pace, you reduce the risk associated with bottlenecks. This is actually one of the primary tenets of the Kanban style of Agile workflows. When too many stories get "stuck" in a particular status and violate the WIP (work in progress) limit for that status, then everyone on the team is expected to pitch in to bring the WIP task count to a reasonable number.

A keen project leader will think about redundancy when the team for the project is being chosen and choose the right balance of resources, with redundant skills to set the project up for success.

I was actually the bottleneck on my own project at several points in my career. This can happen when you hold both leadership as well as individual contributor responsibilities. If you are assuming a project leadership role in addition to your day-to-day work, don't forget to manage yourself as you would any other risk on that project. Remind yourself of the most critical tasks that require your focus, and then work with your sponsor to delegate other tasks to other team members. Don't feel bad for identifying yourself as a risk up front. Do it sooner rather than later so that you can preempt it. Being preventive about it shows maturity, demonstrates that you have self-awareness, and is much better than letting your team down mid-project.

Reduce rollout risk by making changes incrementally

This final type of risk only applies to projects where you are changing an existing process or product that is already live. When you are in this situation, you should work with your team to identify a rollout strategy that reduces impact to the existing users. This is preferred over doing a cutover where the changes are launched to 100 percent of your audience in one "big bang." One option is to phase the releases so that changes happen as small, incremental updates. Alternatively, you can have one big update but only expose it to a percentage of your user base.

As an example, if you are making drastic changes to a tool that is currently used by the sales team, you may want to support the old and new tools in parallel to reduce the risk of failure during your rollout. When the new tool is ready, you may have a set of beta users trying out the new tool before you push it out to the entire sales team and retire the old one. If there is a drastic failure with the new tool, you may have a mechanism to route all of the users back to the old tool quickly to prevent major loss in productivity.

Up-front planning and brainstorming several options and scenarios will be helpful for a safe rollout. Sometimes you get to the finish line and you're so excited to be done that you rush to the end before you are truly ready. Rolling out changes incrementally and carefully, like packing a parachute properly, will help prevent that type of failure.

HOW TO PREEMPT RISK

Plan for overages.
- Build additional time and budget into your overall project timeline if possible. This will allow you to tap into your reserves as a first option when unknowns arise.

Prevent burnout.
- Save heroism for times during the project where hard work is sure to have a major impact.
- Set expectations up front with your team about what you will need.
- Tell them why it is important and how their work made an impact.
- Tend to your team's physical needs by providing food and giving them time to rest after they've worked for an intense stretch.

Identify blind spots.
- Use a premortem to uncover risks.
  - ☐ A premortem is an exercise where you choose a date in the future after the launch and ask the hypothetical question: "Imagine we are now three months out from the launch of this project, and it has failed. What went wrong?"
  - ☐ Use this exercise to crowdsource risks, general concerns, and blind spots.
- Assign biggest risks to the individuals most responsible for that category of work to incorporate into their own plans.
- Write down and publish the results of the premortem and refer back to it often to confirm that risks are being handled properly.
- Add any "missed" stakeholder groups to your overall communications.

Reduce bottlenecks.

- Build a team with redundant skill sets.
- Set the expectation that individuals can and should pitch in to help others.
- Don't forget to manage yourself as a risk if you are an individual contributor and can become a bottleneck.

Make changes incrementally and carefully.

(Only applicable to live features or processes)

- Roll out changes gradually with either smaller feature sets changing, or to portions of your audience at any given time.
- Have a plan in place to roll back or swap out any major changes quickly to reduce negative impact to live users.

◆ ◆ ◆

CHAPTER 9

Why "One-Size-Fits-All" Processes Backfire

People often think that the best project leaders are those who have organized every detail and are always in control. In fact, it's often the opposite. The most effective project leaders are those who direct their teams but relinquish control of the details. They create just enough structure to guide, while instilling a sense of ownership.

They know that inundating their teams with unnecessary processes and checklists in order to feel a sense of control is a sign of weakness. Instead, they have the strength to trust and lean on their teams to get the job done. Strong project leaders personalize the process to the team's needs so they can balance control and autonomy. Using this approach, they produce the best work, with the most efficiency, and have the best time doing the job.

I worked on a site redesign project several years ago where we applied a personalized, lightweight process with success. That project, to date, is still one of the most ambitious and complex projects I've encountered. The scope was to redesign all of the key pages on the website within six months, and the project had a hard deadline. We would lose money if we didn't deliver by January 1 because we were signing contracts that depended on new features being available at that time.

Just three months from the launch date, we uncovered an issue with the architecture that would require the teams to rebuild the pages we had just built in the preceding three months. It was all hands on deck. Every website developer, designer, and product owner was pulled in to work on the project full-time. All told, there were five development teams and numerous other supporting people from stakeholder groups who would need to work together to make it happen—close to one hundred people moving at top speed.

This is a perfect example where too much process or too much planning would have sunk us. The project was moving so fast that it was changing daily. Had we attempted to plan and control every variable, we would have surely stifled the teams and lost our own sanity in the process. What we needed was lightweight project organization that was durable, sustainable, and provided just the right amount of direction and visibility to keep tasks on track. It needed to be easy to understand, easy to access, and easy to maintain. We needed everyone to take full ownership of their tasks and apply their expertise to get things done. We needed people to feel fully invested, to work long hours without complaint, and to communicate well. We didn't have any padding left in our timeline for red tape or big mistakes. The stakes were high, and we knew we had to be precise and swift in our execution.

To ensure success, my executive sponsor and I devised a plan to guide, not control. First, we clearly articulated the goals and the timeline. There was no beating around the bush, just a firm and concise target. Then we collaborated with the leads on each team to tailor the process to this specific project's needs. We moved all the teams into one gigantic room and asked everyone to come to work in person. This was meant to break down any physical and figurative walls that could hinder seamless collaboration among individuals and teams.

Next, we wanted to have a physical representation of account-ability and progress that would live in plain sight so that it could not be missed. We created a whiteboard with a grid of Post-its that we affectionately named the "information radiator." On it, we added notes representing every task to be completed, their assignees, and due dates. The information radiator was proudly displayed in the war room. To incentivize our team members to update it immediately when tasks were completed, we bribed them with $1 lottery tickets that they could claim each time they checked off a task.

On a daily basis, we met for a twenty-minute scrum. Thirty team members, standing in a big circle around the information radiator, reported on progress and called out dependencies and handoffs for the day. Finally, a steering committee met first thing every morning to review new issues that were uncovered, to make quick decisions on scope and trade-offs, as well as refine the process as needed. Outside of that, we chose a common location for all the documents (in Google Drive) and kept detailed task information in JIRA but allowed the stories to be maintained by individual teams.

If you have ever seen a project of this size, you will recognize that this was an insanely light-handed management approach in compar-ison to other projects of similar size and complexity. We didn't have a detailed plan, we didn't micro-manage every action. We articulated clear goals, created two standing meetings, had a way to show clear accountability, and then asked every person on the project to help us by doing what they did best. We guided carefully but then trusted our team to deliver. We reviewed our process regularly and fine-tuned it as we learned more. And we were successful.

The project launched on time and hit its performance metrics. What impresses me most, though, is despite how hard we asked people to work, and how many late hours they pulled, I often hear developers reminiscing about that project in a positive light. They remember how everyone stepped up and bonded over our ability to work together to achieve something big. And they feel proud to have been a part of it.

Was it hard? Yes. Did it often feel like we were on the brink of chaos and failure? Yes. But it was one of the most exciting and rewarding projects I've ever led, and I would do it again in a heartbeat.

Rather than aiming to organize and control my projects, I now aim to "bring order to chaos," similar to how we approached that project. In my experience, the most exhilarating, memorable, and successful projects are those that seem to be teetering on the edge of chaos, but have just enough oversight that the chaos is directed.

The secret to directing chaos with as little overhead as possible is to personalize the process to best serve your specific team and your specific project. Institute only processes that are helpful, and discard any rigidity that does not help. Then, refine them as you learn more about what works best. Like plans, the best organization and process for your project will be lightweight. It will provide the minimum of what your team needs to do their best work. Then, your job is simply to trust and support them.

Define working agreements to source preferences from your team

The beginning of a project is one of the most challenging periods for your team. There is typically a feeling of urgency to get the project off the ground quickly. It is at this point that many traditional project managers will draw from cookie-cutter methodologies and templates to dictate to their teams how the project should be run. By doing so, they are aiming to take control of the project.

But what often happens is that these standard processes will backfire by alienating the team with rules that don't work well for their situation. Just like snowflakes, every project is unique. There are different goals, timelines, personalities, and dynamics. What works well for one team often doesn't work well for others. As a result, when well-intentioned project managers impose rules in an effort to make things better, they often make things worse.

One of the best pieces of advice I've ever read was from an interview with author Debbie Millman, from Tim Ferriss's book *Tribe of Mentors*. She said, "I try to obey this message I got in a Chinese fortune cookie (which I have since taped to my laptop): 'Avoid compulsively making things worse.'"

I often think about this advice when I'm working with my teams. Just because I think a process is good, or it has worked for another team, doesn't mean that it will be helpful to *this* team. Compulsively imposing a process to satisfy my own need for order could do more damage than harm. The best way to know what will work is to actually work with the team to define it.

To that end, I use a method called *working agreements* to personalize processes at the beginning of a project.

When I first started conducting working agreements, I was inspired by a well-known model for group development that was defined by an American psychological researcher named Bryan Tuckman. In his model, he describes the four stages of any new team:

1. **Forming:** The first stage of development occurs when the team initially forms and begins to start working together.
2. **Storming:** The team starts to have some conflict as they learn to work together.
3. **Norming:** The team starts to understand each other and work more harmoniously together.
4. **Performing:** The team reaches a level of maturity in their relationship and begins to exhibit high performance.

My goal for creating working agreements was to bypass the storming phase by getting the team to communicate more before they start working together.

Working agreements are deceptively simple in concept, but I've found them to be exceedingly effective for determining how to best organize a project. To create a working agreement, I pull the team into a meeting and then walk them through a series of questions. The object of the questions is to uncover the team's preferences for working together.

- Is there a person on the team who wakes up late and can't have a coherent conversation until noon? Then you don't want to schedule a scrum at 9:00 a.m.
- Is there a person who always works remotely? Then team meetings will need to be remote-friendly.
- Does everyone hate email and prefer Slack? Then Slack will be the primary mode of communication among team members.

You get the picture. After each question, I let everyone chime in with their opinions, and then I help them decide on conventions they want to use. Once that conversation is done, I codify the agreed terms in writing and immediately begin applying the rules that have been agreed upon.

When I've facilitated these working agreements sessions, I've always received rave reviews. Teams like that it's not a one-size-fits-all approach. Instead, the processes and rules are specifically tailored to the team's needs. The exercise quickly uncovers pet peeves and provides a positive forum for airing them out, which allows everyone to feel heard. The team starts up more quickly and has fewer early conflicts. Their processes run more smoothly because the time was taken to think about them up front, and everyone is fully bought into them. They are left with rules that work well instead of dealing with arbitrary rules that work against them. Finally, the teams are happier and feel a greater sense of ownership because they have been empowered to create an environment that works best for them.

The result of a successful working agreements session is a published document that covers all the basics of project organization. All the big questions are asked and addressed in a fully transparent manner, before any misunderstandings have a chance to develop.

In addition to having a more productive team, there are several other benefits to adopting working agreements for you as the project leader. First, the burden for determining the organizational structure that works best is shifted from you to the team. They decide, you just guide. Second, by identifying and serving your team's needs instead of trying to control them, your team is apt to see you as a better leader.

James Hunter, author of the book *The Servant*, explains this phenomenon: "When you sow service and sacrifice by identifying and meeting needs, you will reap influence. And influence is the essence of leadership." Trust breeds influence. Influence is leadership.

Since I started using working agreements, I learned two things. First, while I thought I was unique by creating working agreements, they are actually widely used by leaders in other companies to help teams avoid potential misunderstandings as they start working together. Atlassian has even published a playbook you can use to create working agreements using their technique, which you can find online at www.atlassian.com/team-playbook/plays/working-agreements. If you want to conduct your own session, you can follow their guide, mine at the end of the chapter, or create your own flavor. The choice is yours. As long as your method helps your team agree on how they will work together, it will be effective.

Second, Tuckman's model, which had inspired my thinking, has been challenged by dozens of researchers who argue that teams don't always transition through the phases linearly. Some researchers believe phases can be skipped; others have extended the number of phases. Yet others have argued that the storming phase often never subsides.

In my own experience, I've also had a hard time cleanly labeling the development stage for any particular team. Every team is different, and the dynamics of the team will often change based on circumstances that impact the people on the team as well as the project. As the people and the project evolves, so do their needs. And therefore, working agreements are never really done. They merely represent what a team thinks will work best at a single point in time. As such, the best working agreements will also evolve alongside the team. You can make sure that they keep up-to-date by revisiting them regularly during retrospectives (which I cover in a later section of this chapter).

Personalize task tracking and workflows to what works best for your team

In addition to creating working agreements, your team will benefit from having a mechanism to track all the work to be done for your project, the relative priorities, assignments, and the workflow. This type of record keeping is helpful to institute if it does not already exist. It will provide transparency into the progress of your project for everyone on the team.

Many tools available have been built expressly for the purpose of tracking tasks and their respective workflows. If you have a small project, you can simply use a spreadsheet. However, if you have a large project with more complexity, a robust tool can be helpful.

If you are struggling to choose a tool, the rule of thumb I use is to adopt the tool that your team likes the most. Getting people to adopt a new process in any scenario is a challenge; you don't need the uphill battle of also convincing them to use a particular tool that they don't like. As with all tools and processes: garbage in means garbage out. The best tool is the one that gets used. Therefore, choose the one that your team is willing to commit to using so that the data that are captured are accurate and complete. Put all your project tasks in that tool and then work with your team to keep the statuses of those tasks up-to-date.

I use the term *workflow* to describe the life cycle of any given task. If you have never used a tool that tracks workflow and you have a longer running project, I recommend that you look into tools that have this function. The simplest tool that I've used is Trello (www.trello .com). It's free to use and easy to set up, but doesn't have any bells and whistles for reporting on progress or velocity. There are many more sophisticated tools you can use (I'm familiar with Asana, Atlassian's JIRA, and Clubhouse, among others) if you require reporting functions, but don't bother unless you need that level of sophistication.

Once you have agreed on a tool, define task statuses as part of your working agreement session. The most straightforward method I've found to determine meaningful statuses is to identify the points in which a task will transition from one person to another. Define statuses in your workflow based on these transitions. Configure the tool you're using to reflect these statuses. When a transition happens for a given task, update the status and assign it to the next responsible person. This will ensure clarity of accountability and also make it clear when a handoff has occurred.

Revisit and refine the process regularly

When you personalize the process for your teams, you're heading into uncharted waters; the process is truly unique to your team, which means no one has tried it before. As a result, it's likely that you will get at least some of it wrong during the first try. Even if you get it right, it's possible your team's needs will change over time. Both of these are good reasons to reflect and refine your process periodically over the course of your project.

A classic method for collaboratively evaluating team performance is to conduct a retrospective. A *retrospective* is just a fancy term for getting the team together and asking them for feedback. It's best to schedule these at some recurring cadence (such as monthly) similar to a regular health checkup. Recurring retrospectives prompt the team to conduct self-reflection and provide an opportunity to discuss feedback from anyone on the team in a constructive manner.

You typically ask three standard questions during a retrospective: (1) What went well? (2) What didn't go well? (3) What should we change? When I do them myself, I like to use a combination of a pre-survey followed up with a meeting to discuss what was written. This method works well for both remote and in-person teams, because it gives people a chance to think about the feedback they want to give on their own time and without the influence of others, and then provides flexibility for them to elaborate on thoughts once they've heard the feedback of their colleagues.

A clever project leader will tailor the wording of each of the questions in the survey to make sure you get the maximum benefit from the exercise. You can also prompt the team for different or additional questions depending on the outcome you seek. I personally always throw in a question that prompts for props or praise for individual team members, because I believe retrospectives are a good tool for reflection and celebration. The right set of questions will make the process collaborative and prompt your team to self-reflect so you can extract both areas for improvement as well as praise.

Like a productive meeting, a productive retrospective is purpose-driven and will result in follow-up items that you act upon to improve how the team is working together. When process changes are agreed upon during a retrospective, then they should get codified in your working agreements document so that it reflects the latest decisions for your evolving team.

I like to use retrospectives to target specific problem areas that I see or hear about from the team. When we're facing a challenge, I bubble it up during the retrospective so that we can have a rich discussion about how to overcome it. When everyone involved is able to contribute to the discussion, they feel a greater sense of control over the outcome and are more invested when we implement any resulting change. This also makes the team more resilient when dealing with any type of change during the project.

Retrospectives are a healthy practice. When paired with a personalized and thoughtful process, they empower your team to create processes that work for everyone involved. They allow you to continually mold your process to boost productivity and create a sense of shared ownership over the outcome.

HOW TO CREATE WORKING AGREEMENTS

Identify your working group.

♦ Schedule a meeting with the group of people who will need to work together. For a big project, you may have multiple working groups and may want to define working agreements for each group. Use your best judgment.

Prepare a list of project organization questions.

♦ Use a basic list of questions but customize the template to include any topics that you know are hot topics that would require some debate.

  ☐ What is our team/project name?
   • Defining a team name can be helpful in establishing a team identity and creating more stickiness.

  ☐ What recurring meetings do we need?
   • What purpose does each serve and who should attend them?
   • Where and what time will we conduct our meetings?
   • What virtual meeting software will we use? (Webex, Google Meet, Zoom, other?)

  ☐ How will we track our work?
   • What methodology should we use? (Waterfall, Agile, Kanban, other?)
   • What tools should we use? (JIRA, Trello, other?)
   • What are the steps in the workflow for each task? (What transitions exist for each task?)
   • How do we define "done" for each task?

  ☐ How will we provide visibility into the progress of our work?
   • What tools will we use? (electronic board, Post-it board, presentation deck, other?)

□ How will we communicate with one another?
  • What communication tools will we use? (Slack, Google Chat, email)
  • What are expected response times for each form of communication?
  • Where will project documentation be kept?
  • Which repositories will we use for each type of document?
□ Are there any special needs/considerations for team members that we need to be aware of? (special working hours, for example)

Walk through the questions.

♦ Schedule a meeting to walk through the questions one by one and discuss the preferences with the team.

♦ Document the answers and any relevant constraints that were used to determine the answers.

♦ Don't rush this process! Take the time needed to discuss the questions in full. Even if it takes two or three meetings to get through the discussion, it will save you time later by preventing future miscommunication.

Publish the agreement.

♦ Once the agreement is done, send it out.

♦ Publish the agreement to make it available publicly so that any person on the team can refer to it when there are differences of opinion.

Support the processes.

♦ Help your team roll out the processes that were decided in the working agreements session.

♦ Assign accountability for any follow-up tasks and take a few organizational tasks on yourself. This may include tasks such as creating Slack channels, updating workflows, and creating document folders.

Review and refine.

- ◆ Schedule time to revisit the working agreements and update them as the team learns more and refines the way they work together over time. This can be done in a recurring meeting (like a retrospective) or as its own ad hoc meeting when you notice conflicts arising intra-team that need to be resolved.

HOW TO RUN A RETROSPECTIVE

Schedule regular retrospectives.
- Schedule retrospectives on a recurring cadence to encourage healthy self-reflection.

Ask questions to prompt self-reflection, both positive and negative.
- Classic questions are these: What went well? What didn't go well? What should we change?
- Customize these questions to your team's personality and add questions to focus on specific problem areas if needed.
- For teams that are shy, consider sending out a survey first to collect responses in writing that you can use to seed a live discussion.

Discuss specific challenges with the group.
- Allow everyone to contribute to the discussions around challenges. Discuss specific examples and brainstorm solutions.
- Agree on action items that can be implemented as a result to improve the process.

Codify changes.
- Codify any changes to the process in your team's working agreements documentation.
- Immediately work with the team to start integrating the changes you agreed upon into your daily process.

PART III

♦ ♦ ♦

How to Support a Project That's in Flight

CHAPTER 10

How Relay Races Are Won (Hint: It's in the Handoffs)

"Project managers are an efficiency, not a necessity." That was my realization after taking lead of the program management team at Edmunds.

When I started working at Edmunds, project managers were required for every project—so much so that we would borrow people from other teams who had the skills to serve in those roles when we had gaps. In more recent times, however, attitudes toward project management had changed. There were many more projects than project managers. And yet, work was still getting done.

It was clear to me that to best serve the company, we had to transcend the idea that project managers were a necessity to every team. Our refined mission was to be a much more targeted task force, to help lead the subset of projects that were high risk, high visibility, or had tight and hard deadlines. Our sweet spot was to work on projects that spanned multiple teams, to be the common thread that would help those teams work together more seamlessly. The goal was to complement current teams and to identify and fill the gaps between them to make all of the teams involved successful. We project leaders were catalysts with the specialized function of making projects move faster. And that is how we added the most value to the company.

Much of the advice from this book is intended to teach you how to personify the same mission we adopted on that program management team, a mission to create efficiency. Regardless of your official title at your company, when you are being asked to lead a project, your primary goal should always be to remove anything that hinders efficiency for your team.

The earlier chapters in this book covered skills, such as creating alignment and laying down structure, that are used to help create efficiency at the beginning of projects. In that phase, you are trying to perform just enough to create a solid foundation for your team to do work. The efficiency you bring is mostly preventive. You ask all the questions that need to be answered to provide clear marching orders and reduce miscommunication down the line. You create an environment where the experts on your team would be able to put their heads down and focus on completing the task at hand.

When you move into the "do work" phase, your role as a project leader changes. The main source of efficiency during project execution is borne of your ability to create seamless transitions.

Consider Olympic relay races. When you are enthralled by a highly competitive relay, and you listen to the commentary from the sports announcers as you watch, you'll notice that they focus a lot on handoffs. This is because highly competitive relay races are won in the transitions between team members. When the baton was handed off, was there a fumble before the next person had a strong grasp of it in their hands? A second or two was lost there. Was the recipient not ready to take the baton? Even worse, several seconds lost. Was the baton dropped? Disastrous, perhaps they lost thirty seconds.

Relay racers know that running fast alone is not enough to win the race. They train heavily on how to make a clean pass. They learn to make sure that they can hold batons at just the right angle so that they can make solid contact with its recipient. They know there is no room for mistakes, because a small fumble can cost them the race.

Projects are much like relays. Tasks are being handed off from one specialist to another all day every day. However, our teams don't often train to make seamless handoffs. Therefore, in each handoff, there is an opportunity to reduce waste and gain time. Where this is especially true is when a handoff occurs between teams that don't work together often. If you are the project leader, this is your sweet spot for adding value in the execution.

As Ray Immelman shares in his book about tribal leadership, *Great Boss Dead Boss*, "Great bosses work to build interfaces between tribes, aligning the system to people until the melding of tribes seems to be the most natural thing." As a watcher over the end-to-end process, you can see in advance when transitions are coming and then provide the help needed to make them happen with as little friction as possible. You can help meld your tribes until the transitions between them are barely noticeable.

When you focus on helping your team in this manner, you will not only increase the throughput for your team, you will also gain more influence. People will clearly see that you are making the project better in its entirety by expediting their handoffs. In his *Inc.* article "34 Things You Need to Give Up to Be Successful," Benjamin Hardy explains that "helping others actually helps you because it makes the system as a whole better. It also builds relationships and trust and confidence." Your team will feel supported, and you will be able to help them meet aggressive goals. And when you are running under a tight deadline, expediting handoffs is what will ultimately help your team win the race.

Translate between people to resolve disconnects

The first tactic for expediting handoffs builds on the skills you developed in chapter 5 to accurately synthesize information. Disconnects between teams are some of the most common gaps that a project leader can fill and are often the cause for botched handoffs. Through the act of synthesis, you can create better connections between people who don't always communicate well by clearly calling out interdependencies between them.

I often sit in meetings during which individuals report their own status but then fail to listen to what others report. People are always busy. They may be on their laptop, working and responding to emails, trying to squeeze in a little work while sitting in the meeting. As a result, they are only partially present. In those discussions, I will hear pieces of information they miss. When that happens, I make it a point to paraphrase the point I heard, call the name of the person who I believe needs that information the most, and then make a statement about the impact specifically to that person. My goal is to make sure the person who needs the information the most hears it and acknowledges it. Then I give them a chance to react.

EXAMPLE 1

- Lee: "I'll be on vacation next week."
- Maria: "I need Lee to complete this task within the next week or else I will be blocked."
- You (synthesis): "Lee, it sounds like Maria needs your task completed by this week. Is that doable before you leave for vacation? If not, can you suggest an alternative."
- Lee: "Yes, actually I think I can have it done this week if we can prioritize the second item Maria asked for. Is that okay for you, Maria?"
- Maria: "Yes that works."
- Lee: "Okay great, I'll hand it off to you this week."
- Maria: "I'll watch for it."

By using this technique, you can make sure both parties have the same expectations for their interdependent work.

People from different teams are also prone to talk past each other. I notice this often if I am listening closely enough—two different people may use the same word but that word has a different meaning to each person. The best way to catch these disconnects is to tell myself a story in a sequence, considering dependencies I've gleaned from previous conversations.

EXAMPLE 2

- Martin from the sales team: "We will be launched by Friday."
- Kim from the operations team: "We will be launched by Friday."
- You (synthesis): "I believe the sales contract needs to be signed before the operations team can be done with their work. Martin, when you say that you will be launched, does that mean the contracts will be signed or something else? Kim, when you say you will be launched, are you leaving enough time to do the configuration that needs to be done until after the contract is signed by Martin's team?"
- Martin: "Our contracts will be signed on Friday."
- Kim: "After we get the contracts from you, Martin, we'll need another week to finish configuration."
- You (synthesis): "That means that we will be fully launched next Friday instead of this Friday, correct?"
- Martin and Kim: "That's correct."

When you use this technique, you will need to faithfully represent the opinions and information as they are stated. While you do want to attempt to draw the conclusions, the inputs should not be cluttered by your own opinion. You are a mediator, connecting two parties. To have credibility in that role, people must trust you to understand their words and paraphrase properly. When you do it correctly, you will succeed in expediting the proper handoff between the two teams and also earn some appreciation for clearing up misconceptions about dependent work.

Route handoffs to reduce gaps between tasks

Once dependencies are clearly articulated and acknowledged, you want transitions to happen as quickly as possible. Between a task being completed and being picked up by the next person in the relay, there is always a pause. Reducing the length of that pause will improve your overall completion time.

Author Madeleine L'Engle introduced a wonderful metaphor for how to gain efficiency in her classic story, *A Wrinkle in Time.* In the book, a scientist explains that people think of time on a continuum, like an extended piece of rope. However, "A straight line is not the shortest distance between two points." You can time travel by creating a "wrinkle" or a fold in the rope to shorten it.

When you expedite handoffs, you are doing something similar to time traveling by shortening the overall time it takes to complete a task. You can shorten time by reducing the pauses, essentially creating your own folds in the overall timeline. To do it, learn each person's role and area of expertise. Having that knowledge will allow you to understand the best person to receive each handoff. You want to brace both the person sending as well as receiving for the exact point in time when the handoff will occur. Then, when a person is ready to hand off, you tag the person receiving the handoff to reduce any pause in the transition. With this approach, you create your own "wrinkle in time" by removing the pause.

Let's continue the conversation between Martin and Kim from our sales and operations team a few days later.

EXAMPLE 3

- You: "Martin, are you still on track to complete the contracts by Friday?"
- Martin: "Yes."

- You (routing): "Kim, Martin's team will hand off the contracts to you by Friday. Will you have a person ready on your team to start working on the configuration?"
- Kim: "Yes, I'll make sure that Camille is ready."
- You (routing): "Camille, Martin and I will let you know as soon as the contracts are ready so that you can get started."
- Camille: "Great. Thanks."

From this conversation, you know the exact timing for the hand-off and the person to tag when it's done. The only thing left to do is watch for the signal from Martin that his team is done, and then tag in Camille.

This technique does not have to be used all the time. In fact, if it is overused, it will feel like micro-management. However, when you are under a tight timeline, it's effective and appreciated. Without tagging Camille to do her piece, the finished contracts might sit for hours or potentially over the weekend before she sees them. When you call her out specifically, you'll reduce the length of the gap between teams and save that time overall.

Even more efficiency can be gained when there are multiple tasks, culminating into a single handoff. As an example, most restaurant kitchens have multiple stations cooking individual dishes that have to be assembled onto the same plate before being handed off to the server to serve to the customer. Restaurants know that having a person manning the intersection to make sure the sides come together with the main course is the most efficient way to get a completed plate to the server. Your role as a project leader is to bring the same efficiency to your project by sitting at the intersection of multiple tasks and bundling them for handoff when they are ready.

Remove blockers to keep work flowing efficiently

A third method for expediting handoffs is to help clear blockers. A *blocker* is just a fancy term for a handoff that is taking longer than expected.

In his book *The Hard Thing about Hard Things*, technology entrepreneur Ben Horowitz shares an insightful observation about blockers that I've also found to be true in my own experience. He said, "An early lesson I learned in my career was that whenever a large organization attempts to do anything, it always comes down to a single person who can delay the entire project. An engineer might get stuck waiting for a decision or a manager may think she doesn't have authority to make a critical purchase. These small, seemingly minor hesitations can cause fatal delays."

When an important piece of your project is blocked, you have the power to unblock it by working to rapidly identify the source. Discover the person who is the key to resolving the issue, and then work to clear up any misalignments.

In most cases, the blockage will be caused by a prioritization issue. I see this often when the person is shared across multiple projects and doesn't have the right context. He is unable to choose which task is most important and, therefore, may make the wrong decision. By reaching out to him and making a clear request, you can typically unblock the issue quickly. Remember to provide a clear what, when, and why. For example, "Marco, my team is waiting on you to finish updating the data so that they can start development. They are currently blocked. It is important that we get started as soon as possible because we have an aggressive deadline and have to finish the code tomorrow. Our head of sales has requested that we expedite this because he believes our client will cancel the contract if we miss. Can you find time to help us today?"

Often, making a clear request and providing the appropriate context will be enough for Marco to act. However, there will be some cases where your urging is not enough. In that case, you will need to call on your sponsor to work with Marco's boss to agree to a delivery date. Escalation is a last resort, but is effective if you need the task done quickly.

Plug gaps to help your team and gain respect

The final way to expedite handoffs is to plug gaps during transitions if you have the skill to do so. One common failure of project managers that I've seen is a refusal to step outside of their "assigned" responsibilities in order to help out the team in a pinch. A project leader doesn't stay within the lines. She knows her ultimate job description is to do "whatever the team needs in order to deliver the project" and is willing to roll up her sleeves if the need arises. It is precisely her willingness to act in this way that garners her the most respect from her team. When she plugs gaps, she literally becomes glue for her team.

On my own projects, stepping in to help out when the team is in need has also given me the opportunity to learn new skills. Because of my desire to always help when I can, I pick up skills on every project. I'm often called a "Jack-of-all-trades" because I can manage projects, write stories, test stories, debug work, write documentation, query data—whatever skill is needed that I can learn, I do the best I can to learn it.

My husband, who worked in restaurants during college, often likens how I see my role to a general manager at a restaurant. General managers are in charge of making sure the restaurant operates well by managing the people and all the processes at a restaurant. As a part of their training, general managers are required to learn how to work all the stations so that they can step in when an employee is unexpectedly unavailable, and a replacement can't be found quickly. As a result, a GM can be a host or hostess, a line cook, work the salad station, and bus or wait tables if needed. The GM may not be able to plug the gap of an expert like the head chef, but can do many tasks reliably enough to keep the restaurant in operation in most cases when there is an unexpected vacancy.

A project leader will aim to do the same for her project. For example, if a developer has completed his task but requires a person to test it before it can get deployed, she will pitch in to help further testing progress instead of just waiting.

Effective project leaders make sure that important tasks that need to be handed off do not sit idle. Even if you cannot fully complete the task yourself, there is typically some way you can either pitch in or find help to drive some progress. Helping one person will ultimately help the system as a whole. And your team will appreciate you for it.

HOW TO EXPEDITE HANDOFFS

Call out handoffs before they happen.
- Synthesize conversations between teams and raise interdependencies when you believe they exist.
- Call on people by name and state how they will be affected.
- Wait for acknowledgment that they understand the role they will play.

Route handoffs to the next person.
- When an important handoff is coming, know who it is coming from, who it will be going to, and the exact timing for the transition.
- Watch for the completion of the first task and then tag the person with the next task as soon as it's ready.

Remove blockers that are delaying handoffs.
- All blockers can be tracked down to a person. Identify the source of the blocker.
- Make a clear request that includes what you need, when you need it, and why it is important. Then, get a commitment on a date to deliver.
- If you are unable to clear up the blocker this way, escalate to a sponsor who will have more formal authority to clarify priorities.

Plug gaps that are causing delays in handoffs.
- Pitch in where you can or find someone who can help. This will make you feel more integrated with the team and also give you the chance to learn new skills.
- If you can't fully plug the gap yourself, you can at least help to make progress on it so that the dependency does not sit idle.

CHAPTER 11

Three Levers to Keep Your Project On Time and On Budget

I have never led a project that has obediently stayed on track from start to finish. Leading a project has always felt more like watching a pilot steer a plane in unpredictable weather. The pilot starts with a solid takeoff and a flight path to a clear destination. But once off the ground, the pilot must do a lot of maneuvering as the weather conditions change to keep course. If there is an obstacle, the pilot must adjust the plane's path to avoid it. If there are headwinds, the pilot must increase acceleration to overcome it. If there is a storm, the pilot must make in-the-moment choices between speed, altitude, and safety to minimize turbulence.

The best pilots know that the flight path will have unknowns, but they also have the right skills to adjust to those unknowns as they arise.

Similarly, all projects are guaranteed to be fraught with unknowns that threaten to derail them. To make it to your destination gracefully (instead of crashing and burning), like a skilled pilot, you must become comfortable with managing in-the-moment trade-offs that balance the needs of your project. You have three main levers at your disposal to manage issues: scope, time, and resources.

To keep on course, you will want to be well versed with explaining and negotiating trade-offs among these three constraints within the context of your project.

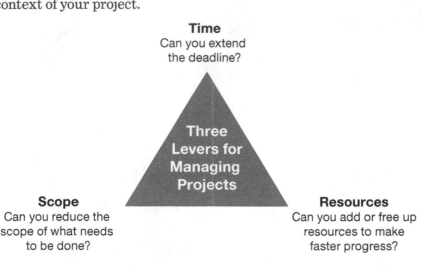

The three project levers.

On every project you lead, you will encounter choices that need to be made to balance scope, time, and resources. As an example, when I initially started writing this book, I planned for only thirteen chapters. But as I started writing, I found chapters missing from the outline that I wanted to include (introducing my own scope creep). I had to decide whether I should include them or cut others to make room for them (in other words, adjust scope), work longer hours (adding resources), or extend my timeline. I had to make decisions about which services to do myself versus hiring out for editing and publishing (managing resources). I had to constantly ask myself what was most important to me so that I could focus on the task at hand (prioritizing my work).

Rather than dreading trade-offs, I have come to welcome them. When I work with my teams and am forced to make trade-offs, we are able to zero in even further on what's most important to the success of each project. Any elasticity that exists at the beginning of the project is reduced by the choices you make as the project progresses. As a result, the more choices you are required to make, the more clarity you gain, and the greater your ability to focus your team toward the finish line.

In the coming sections, I talk about strategies for managing trade-offs with the three levers—scope, time, and resources. The goal is to prepare you to balance these trade-offs when challenges arise.

Manage trade-offs with time

The easiest lever to move when something doesn't go as planned is *time*. "We need to add something, can we?" "Sure, that can be done. We just need to extend the timeline." I started my career in information technology consulting and know too well that a clever consultant will tell you that practically anything is possible given enough time and money. That's because it's a consultant's job to upsell you. However, adding time is a slippery slope.

I've seen this happen over and over again—a big project gets kicked off and is only two weeks from being launched when suddenly the team discovers a problem or a new feature that is now critical to the success of the project. To accommodate the changes, the timeline is extended another three months. Then when the project is down to that last two weeks, another new issue mysteriously appears and the launch is pushed again.

This is a dangerous spiral. I've seen more projects fail after an initial timeline extension than I can count. Extensions in timelines are also typically accompanied by additional budget. So when you extend, you risk failing on two dimensions of your project. You will let your sponsor and your company down if your project runs too long. If your project gets pushed out too many times, it will likely get canceled. You will fail, your team will also fail. Everyone will be discouraged and feel their efforts have gone to waste. That's not the result you want to see for all your hard work.

Are there instances where it is appropriate to add time? Yes, absolutely, but you must be judicious when you add time. The extension must be well worth the trade. For example, if you are building a new product and have received customer feedback that has you absolutely convinced that it will fail without the addition *and* you also have some leeway on the due date, you can extend the timeline to cover the additional scope. Just make sure that this is the exception and that you have full buy-in from your sponsor on the change.

Another example when it is reasonable to add time is when you have an expert who needs to complete work for your project who is not available at the exact time you need them. This may be because the expert is working on something more important than your project (your sponsor should confirm that), or becomes unexpectedly unavailable (due to illness or personal emergencies). If your project can stomach the wait, then you can extend the timeline. Again, I caution against this unless it feels absolutely necessary and everyone has signed off. Effective project leaders typically find other ways to save time by doing work in parallel, expediting handoffs, or finding other means to negotiate around delays in order to deliver on time. Resources and scope are other levers to pursue.

Manage trade-offs with resources

If you don't want to extend your project timeline (and you should not), the next option to explore is whether or not it is possible to add resources to accommodate the change. I use the term *resources* to describe both people and money.

On every project, there are going to be unknowns that you *know* are coming. You may not know exactly what surprises await, but you can bet that something will come up that will require more resources. If you are kicking off a project with a fixed budget, the best method for finishing on budget is to build that risk into your plan up front. Estimate your project budget but add reserve funds to cover the fact that you know unknowns will arise. Then you can use reserve funds when an issue that you didn't originally account for arises. Similarly, if your project has a fixed team, then you should reserve time from at least one person allotted to attack those unknowns.

Some managers may have an aversion to a preemptive approach with budgeting. They might view it as unnecessary padding. Planning for something you know is going to happen is not padding, it's wisdom. If you need to keep your project on time and on budget, you need the means to handle situations you know you were unable to predict at the start of the project.

If you've already exhausted your reserves, then you'll need to negotiate an acceptable solution. Can you get an additional person to work on this newly uncovered, critical feature? And can it be done in parallel with in-flight work streams? If so, you can try to obtain approval for the incremental budget to add resources. If the expert is not available, who is the next best person to do the job? Is she working on something more important? Can you get her instead? Always explore these options before extending the timeline.

I would also recommend being judicious about adding resources. An overrun, over-budgeted project is not generally viewed as a success. So you will want to be careful when you use this lever too.

Manage feature scope

The final lever for keeping projects on track, and the one that I use most widely on my projects, is scope. I use the term *scope* to refer to anything that requires work or resources on your project. In other words, scope is what you need to get done.

Feature scope creep, or the addition of any incremental work in the way of incremental or padded features, is common. For example, if you are working on a project to redesign a single web page, an example of feature scope creep would be when the redesign expands to encompass pages that customers will encounter before or after navigating to that page. With my home renovation project, my original requirement was to make sure we had at least two bathrooms for our family of four. Our contractor upsold us on additional features, somehow ultimately convincing us that we needed four bathrooms, one per person.

The good news is that on every project I've led, scope has never been truly fixed. That makes it a powerful lever because you can almost always cut scope enough to accommodate necessary changes under the desired timeline.

Scope can always be negotiated. It is just a matter of uncovering the most important features for your project and then stopping work on the features that are the least necessary. As Steve Jobs is famously quoted as saying, "People think focus means saying yes to the thing you've got to focus on. But that's not what it means at all. It means saying no to the hundred other good ideas that there are. You have to pick carefully. I'm actually as proud of the things we haven't done as the things I have done. Innovation is saying no to 1,000 things." Your job is to help your team say no.

You may not have the ability to unilaterally make a decision to say no to a particular change yourself but you can help your team choose. To do so, you first need clear, unambiguous goals (which you've thankfully already set at this point). Next, you can provide them a decision-making framework to help them rank the work by relative importance.

When you're working on a personal project such as a wedding or a home renovation, the best method for prioritizing work is simply by preference. Work with your sponsors to enumerate all the items that cost money or extend time, and then force rank them in order. When you do this, you create visibility into exactly how many items are on the list that they *will* get. The ones at the bottom of the list start to feel easier to chop.

When setting feature priorities for a product development project, consider, primarily, these two dimensions: speed and impact. Depending on the phase of your project, what you are measuring for speed and what you are measuring for impact may be different.

In the early phases of your project, learning is often the most important, as learning will play a key role in what you plan to build. Therefore, you'll prioritize tests that will give you the ability to learn the most quickly. When you are building a brand new product, growth potential is typically the main driver for what to do first. Therefore, you'll want to prioritize products with the highest potential impact to growth that you can get into market the fastest.

Once your project has launched, and bugs or iterative enhancements need to be prioritized, then the biggest concern is typically user impact. Bugs that impact the highest number of users will usually also translate to those that have the biggest impact on revenue. Therefore, you'll want to tackle the issues that impact the most users that you can resolve the fastest first.

Finally, if you are working to optimize or stabilize a project that has already launched, you will want to weigh the risks or savings you

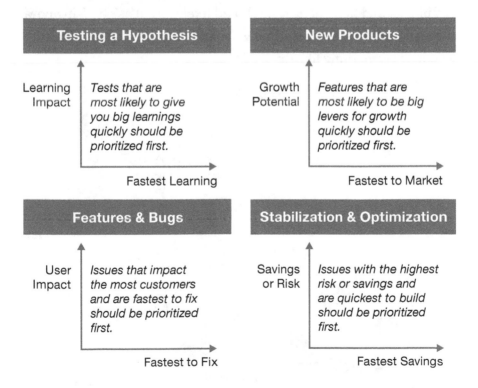

Speed vs. impact types.

can gain from the proposed updates against the time to get those gains.

Once you have determined what you are measuring for speed and for impact, then there are two methods that are useful to try depending on your team's style. The first is the most lightweight, but requires Post-it notes and a wall. I love Post-it notes, so that is my preferred method if I can get people to collaborate on the priorities in person.

To prioritize the work, you just write down all the ideas and then plot them on a grid that has speed on a vertical axis and impact on the horizontal axis. The items in the upper right-hand corner are those that are both fastest and have the highest impact. You should always do those first. The ones to the left that have impact but may take longer should be prioritized next. The ones that have low impact but are fast are perfect for product backlogs, so that they can be pulled in anytime you have some extra time. And finally, the items that have low impact and take a long time should likely be put aside. Using now, soon, and later labels like we did when creating a fuzzy roadmap, the grid looks something like this:

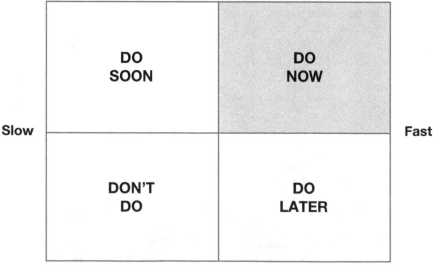

Prioritization grid.

If you are not a fan of Post-it notes or this visual method for prioritization, another option is to create a spreadsheet and provide a simple weighted formula to help your team set priorities. You must choose weights that make the most sense to you. I advise that you decide which dimension is more important—speed or impact—and then slightly handicap the one that is less important. That will help reduce the number of features that have the same overall score. Here's an example:

Feature	Speed	Speed score	Impact	Impact score	Overall score
Feature 1	Fast	8	High	10	18
Feature 2	Medium	4	High	10	14
Feature 3	Slow	0	High	10	10
Feature 4	Fast	8	Medium	5	13
Feature 5	Medium	4	Medium	5	9

Prioritization formula format.

Once you have the weighted list, sort them in descending order of the overall score to make it easy for everyone to see which items have been deemed the least important. I find this method is transparent and most effective with analytical decision-makers.

Choose the method that works best for your team. Each method has advantages and disadvantages, but the main point is to help your team reach more clarity on the importance of particular features.

Once you have the features ranked by importance, then you can discuss the lowest priority items with your team leads to garner agreement on what to cut from scope for your launch. Rather than saying no entirely, you can put these into a Fast-Follow or Phase 2 of your project so that you can prioritize them post-launch. You'd be surprised how much more malleable priorities become when success is near. The closer you get to your launch date, the more people will be willing to compromise on what is required for a launch versus a nice-to-have. I lovingly refer to the items that get cut out of scope at near the very end of the project as *roadkill*. Having a bucket to catch items that will go in the second phase of your project will be extra handy when your roadkill starts to pile up.

Manage implementation scope

A second category of scope is often overlooked that I call implementation scope. This is additional work that may be hidden in the way that your team decides to fulfill a particular function or feature.

For example, if you have a leak in the roof of your home, your contractor may notice that your roof is old and provide you a quote to replace it. If you press further, though, you may find that you can patch the hole now for a lower cost, which will allow you to extend the wear of your roof for a few more years. Inevitably, you will have to replace it, but that could be Phase 2. The original recommendation to replace the roof right away was more than was truly needed and therefore implementation scope.

Well-meaning product owners often do the same thing when defining the specifics of a feature. Experienced engineers will also do this when estimating the build-out of a feature. They will often inflate the scope in order to future-proof it. Often, a simpler implementation will serve as an acceptable patch. However, you may not find the simpler solution unless you ask directly: "Is there a short-term solution we can implement to meet this spirit of the requirement? Can the logic or implementation be simplified in any way to get the feature out sooner?"

When your team is asked to be more flexible and creative for defining a solution that can be done with less effort, they will often succeed. You just need to encourage that discussion.

The objective is not to cut so much scope that your goals cannot be met, but to find work-arounds that are acceptable to everyone while keeping the goals in mind. Everything else can happen after you hit your goals, by moving it to the next phase for your project.

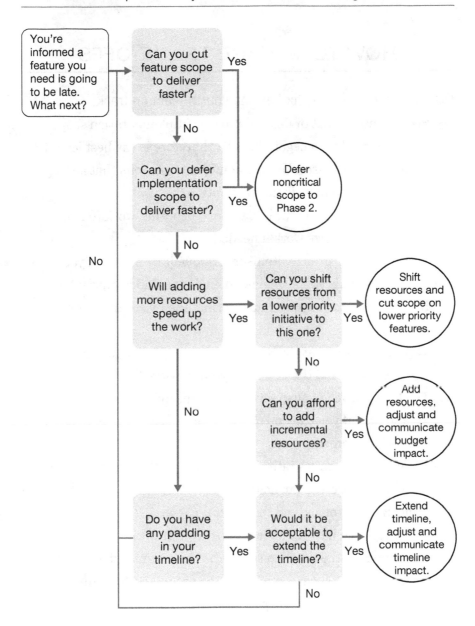

Trade-offs decision tree.

HOW TO MANAGE TRADE-OFFS

Discuss various options for keeping your project on track.
- Scope: Can you cut or defer feature or implementation scope?
  - □ Scope is always negotiable and therefore is the best lever to use in most cases. Use it when it's not obvious that adding time or resources is the best option.
  - □ Discuss speed versus impact for upcoming work to help teams prioritize work if needed.
  - □ Place lower priority items in a queue for Phase 2 of your project. This will also make it easier to find compromises.
- Resources: Can you speed up the timeline by adding more resources?
  - □ Plan a reserve at the beginning of the project for known unknowns and then exhaust your reserve first.
  - □ Once you've exhausted your reserve, add resources sparingly and only if you can add those resources in parallel to current work streams.
  - □ Adding resources rather than just crunching the timeline will help prevent burnout.
- Time: Should you extend the timeline?
  - □ Unless you have a buffer built into your project, extending the timeline should be the last resort. Only do it if it is critical and acceptable to extend the timeline to accommodate an unexpected change.

Choose the option that best supports the business outcomes and team morale.
- After weighing the various trade-off options available, work with your team leads and your executive sponsor to choose the option that best meets the business needs, while keeping team morale
- Your job is to balance both delivery and team happiness.

Communicate the agreement and impact broadly.

- Once you've agreed on which trade-off you will choose, document and communicate the decision and reasoning broadly.
- Do not forget to capture deferred scope for the next phase of your project. This is especially important when it comes to implementation scope when you've negotiated a short-term solution to meet your deadline.

CHAPTER 12

Negotiate Like a Pro,
Even If You Hate Negotiating

I hate negotiating. I'm the type of person who lets her mom negotiate for her at the Asian mall. If my mom isn't with me, then I'll willingly pay full price on an item when I know I probably don't have to, just so that I can avoid the pain of negotiating. Sometimes the shop owner will look at me, take pity, and drop the price anyway just because she can tell I want to avoid bargaining.

When I started working for Edmunds, I realized I was also a target customer for several of their products. Edmunds creates content and products to help customers negotiate better deals for the purchase or lease of a car. Normally, I try to use the products myself, but then am still reluctant to take the plunge to talk to a dealer. (I try to get my husband to do it instead.)

Interestingly, I had a breakthrough a couple of years ago. As a part of customer research work I was doing for one of my projects, I had the pleasure of negotiating a car lease for an Edmunds customer. At first I was intimidated and worried that I might get her an unfavorable deal. However, using Edmunds's tools, I was able to get the dealer to agree to a fantastic price for our customer. She had a wonderful experience with the dealer who honored the exact price I had negotiated, drove the car home, and was so ecstatic that she sent me a photo and thanked me for my efforts. I was so proud of myself.

I had always wondered why I often avoided negotiations in real life, because I was able to negotiate often and well during work while I was leading projects. After my successful car negotiating experience, it dawned on me that I was capable of negotiating well when I was helping others do it because I was not an invested party myself. When I'm negotiating for myself, I have a certain amount of emotional baggage I carry with me into the negotiation. However, when I'm negotiating on behalf of others, I remove myself from that emotional context. Instead, I focus on helping both parties overcome their own emotional baggage to arrive at an agreeable solution. And that's what negotiation on projects is about—finding the best outcome for everyone involved in order to support the collective goals for the team.

In *The Only Negotiating Guide You'll Ever Need,* authors Peter B. Stark and Jane Flaherty share the secret to a successful negotiation. They said, "The ideal outcome for almost all negotiations is win-win. The needs and goals of both parties are met, so they both walk away with a positive feeling—and a willingness to negotiate with each other again."

When I negotiate toward an outcome for my projects, I always aim for win-win solutions. If I start with that state of mind, then the act of negotiation becomes a team bonding event. I guide the team to put aside differences and work together for the common good. We aim to find a solution that works well for everyone, not just one party. In the process, we build trust and strengthen our working relationships. That lays the foundation for easier negotiations in the future and creates a more cohesive team.

To negotiate well, you must have a certain amount of optimism heading into the discussion that a happy outcome can be achieved. When I begin negotiating for a project, I start with the belief that an agreement will be reached—it may just take a little time to brainstorm options that will work.

Negotiation is a core skill that project leaders use to keep their projects on track. Often, teams will get blocked when they can't independently arrive at an agreement. Your job is to clear all blockers, and negotiating an outcome is the only path through this type of blocker. If you, like me, are sometimes shy about negotiating for yourself, don't fret. In the next few sections, I'll provide a few techniques to help you embrace this skill.

Uncover constraints so that you can deal with them

Part of the reason that I'm timid when negotiating for myself is that I carry emotional baggage into the conversation. I don't like feeling wrong or dumb. I fear a certain amount of rejection, and I detest unproductive conflict. Your team members will bring a similar amount of baggage to your discussions. So the first thing you want to do when you prepare for a negotiation is to create a nonthreatening environment to discuss the challenges people are silently holding onto.

Start by asking each person in your negotiation to vocalize their concerns or constraints, participate actively by asking questions, and capture what they have said in writing either on a board or in a document. The point is to make sure that each party feels fully heard.

In *Never Split the Difference*, FBI negotiator Chris Voss shares his wisdom on this topic: "Psychotherapy research shows that when individuals feel listened to, they tend to listen to themselves more carefully and to openly evaluate and clarify their own thoughts and feelings. In addition, they tend to become less defensive and oppositional and more willing to listen to other points of view, which gets them to the calm and logical place where they can be good *Getting to Yes* [another excellent book] problem solvers."

Thus, the best way to set the stage for a productive conversation is to listen and to make everyone feel that you have fully acknowledged their position. There is no better way to do that than to ask questions and to take great notes (which you already know how to do).

When you are taking notes and paraphrasing, state what you've heard simply and accurately, representing each person's point of view without judgment. Just because views are different, it doesn't mean that either person is wrong. You must believe that each person at the table has the best intentions and valid reasons for their resistance. Representing what they have said accurately will get your team to trust that you are aiming to help them with the negotiation, not bully them.

Sometimes differences in opinion seem as if they are being caused by stubbornness, but when you discuss them, you will realize there is a different underlying cause such as culture. In his TED Talk "Weird, or Just Different?" Derek Sivers shares an example of how addresses are assigned differently in the United States versus Japan.

In the United States, we have addresses named by streets and the house numbers incrementally in order from one corner to another. In Japan, streets are not named. Instead, blocks are named and the houses are numbered in the order they are built. In fact, the two countries have a completely opposite way of thinking that makes logical sense in each culture, but baffle a foreigner. If a person from Japan disagrees with a person in the US on how an address should be defined, neither person is wrong, they just have a different approach based on their own prior experiences.

When you listen without judgment, you start to see the hidden causes of differences are not typically stubbornness but borne out of an experience that is valid and should be considered as a part of the final solution.

Summarizing what you've heard in your own words can also make those concerns more understandable to the other parties at the table. Many impasses are caused by lack of understanding between parties. Since you act as a neutral party in the negotiation, you can close the gap of understanding by translating the concern into words that can be universally understood by everyone.

You can also use this neutral position to call out commonalities in the opinions rather than just differences, which will help people see that they are not always adversaries in the negotiation after all. Identifying commonalities is a gluing function because it brings people closer to one another. For example, if I heard a person from the US arguing with a person from Japan on how to define an address, I might say, "What I hear is that you both agree that addresses are useful to help people label where homes reside. We just need to agree on a convention that makes sense for both of you on how to define the addresses. Is that correct?"

Overcome fear of failure through assumptions

Another common source of tension that hinders agreement is an underlying fear of failure. The person who is resisting may be aiming to protect themselves from committing to an inaccurate answer or they may be protecting their team from having to deal with an error in their own decision-making. I see this happen often with people who are extremely intelligent. They are so smart that they can outthink themselves from any solution and, as a result, are reluctant to commit to any particular path.

I once worked with a technical lead who rarely made any firm commitments to anyone at the company. He was the type of person who was so smart that it always felt like you were playing an advanced game of chess rather than having a cordial debate with him. Instead of thinking three steps ahead the way chess players are trained to, he was also thinking three steps backward and questioning any assumptions that had been made to that point. It often felt impossible to win any discussion with him because he could always poke holes in your logic, which was frustrating to our leadership and the team. No doubt it was frustrating to him too. He was so afraid to be wrong and fail that many decisions came to a standstill, and that ultimately created a lot of conflict internally on projects with him. But he was a subject matter expert, and we wanted to include him in discussions to get the best information.

The first time I was asked by my boss to work with our technical lead to get estimates for an upcoming project, I approached him gingerly about it because I knew he would be a reluctant participant. We had a solid working relationship, and I'd seen how he resisted inquisition on a number of occasions, so I knew I wouldn't be able to coerce responses out of him. Instead of trying to debate with him, I decided to first ask him a lot of questions and listen. Then, I paraphrased what I heard back to him and captured it in writing.

Next, I needed to get estimates. When I asked directly for an estimate on a particular task, he would cite multiple reasons why any attempt at an estimate was wrong. I had to change my strategy. To get him to overcome his fear of committing to a wrong answer, I started looking through the fears he had shared and asking him to make assumptions for a "happy path" to get around them. For example, if there was no way we could proceed until we knew how long a client would take to return information to us, I asked him to assume the most common turnaround time for a client. We captured that assumption and then completed the estimate for that task. We walked through each task like that—taking a concern, building in an assumption, and providing an estimate based on the assumption—until we finally had an estimated plan.

When I shared the plan with my boss, he was pleasantly surprised by my success in the conversation. I shared with him what I felt made the negotiation a success: first, my genuine interest in hearing concerns and, second, the use of assumptions for each estimate. The plan adequately captured our technical lead's concerns and provided caveats to alleviate his fear of being wrong. It was a successful negotiation to an outcome, and it also made my working relationship with that technical lead better from that point forward.

Outline possible solutions to gain buy-in

When there are multiple parties in the negotiation and differences of opinion are strong, then I find it best to try to capture various options to solve the problem. This tactic is both nonthreatening and noncommittal. No one has to agree on whether the possible solutions are good or bad when you are outlining them. This allows people to share their ideas without feeling that they will be attacked and lays the foundation for a positive discussion. Outlining possible solutions will get people focused on what *is* possible, rather than on what is not possible. When I am hearing a lot of statements that start with "We can't," I use this tactic to shift the discussion to what we *can* do.

For example, if you are in a room with two parties arguing because they have a difference of opinion, you can interject to defuse conflict by paraphrasing what you're hearing as possible solutions. An example: "I believe what I'm hearing is that Cory is suggesting an option to do X, while Joseph is suggesting an option to do Y. Is that correct?" Capture the possible solutions in writing so that both Cory and Joseph feel like you have acknowledged their opinions. Open a discussion to flesh out each opinion with more details, then ask for more options. Often, just starting the conversation around different options will spur creativity and yield additional solutions that achieve a middle ground.

Once you have a list of possible solutions, discuss pros and cons for each solution. Capture these as well. Then once you've thoroughly discussed all the pros and cons, review the options as a group to determine if one solution is obviously better than the others. Ask each person to vote on their top two choices to identify a clear winner. You may find that it becomes less subjective once you've talked through each option, and that people on your team come to a natural consensus through this exercise.

At this point, your hope is that you will close the deal by coming up with a single recommendation that everyone can stand by and feels meets their individual needs. If that does not happen, get a tie breaker to help push you to a conclusion. When I am still at a standstill, I call on my project sponsor to make the final decision. Presenting options this way makes it easy for a sponsor to evaluate the choices and provide guidance on how to proceed.

Negotiating outcomes by exploring options garners full buy-in on the final decision from everyone involved. In *The Great CEO Within*, Matt Mochary shares that participation in the outcome is the best path to getting people on board with a decision. He said, "You create buy-in when you make people feel that they are part of the decision and that their input contributes to the final outcome. The more influence they feel they have on the outcome, the more they'll be invested in the final result."

Even when a tie breaker is required, the process of identifying options wins buy-in because everyone feels that we did a thorough assessment, treated them with respect, and came to a decision fairly.

When all else fails, negotiate for compliance

In rare cases, no matter what diplomatic tactic I've tried with my team, it is not possible to collaboratively negotiate a solution that meets the original goals. This situation usually happens when there is misalignment; the teams don't agree on what they are being asked to do, and they disagree with the mandate from our project sponsor.

I recently experienced a deadlock during a project that was being requested by a client. Unfortunately, this client had a bad reputation with the teams by being notoriously demanding and often requested custom solutions that were difficult to maintain. Two teams needed to collaborate so we could fulfill the latest "unreasonable" request, and neither of them wanted to do it. They repeatedly resisted no matter how I posed the request, and I couldn't even get them to begin to discuss possible solutions because they were so opposed.

Regardless of how the teams felt, it was up to me to get the job done. The client was an important strategic partner for the company, and we were under direct orders from our sponsor to make it happen. To make progress, I had to abandon a fully collaborative approach for a moment and negotiate for compliance. I would need to use force and authority to get them past their objections so that we could move into a more collaborative stage.

I could have just shoved it down their throats by using the directive I had been given from my executive sponsor to escalate to their bosses and get a direct order they would have to follow. However, I wanted to act in a way that made my team feel respected, not bulldozed. I also needed to preserve a positive working relationship with them for future projects.

In *Never Split the Difference,* FBI negotiator Chris Voss suggests an unusual technique that works well for this type of scenario when you know that your counterparts are going to hate what you have to say but you have to find a way to get them to agree with you anyway. The technique is called an *accusation audit.* You essentially preface the discussion with all of the horrible things that people are thinking in order to reduce the sting of the accusations that are stewing silently in their minds. By saying these accusations out loud first, you acknowledge you've heard the concerns, and you also defuse the power they hold over the accuser.

So I began: "I know that you do not like working with this client. I've heard that the implementation will be suboptimal and difficult to maintain. I know that you are busy and there are a hundred other items on your roadmap that you would rather be doing." I acknowledged, "However, we are being asked to get this done because this client is a strategic partner to us. Our sponsor is asking us to find a way. Can we please move past the objections and collaborate together on the least offensive solution?"

They didn't like what I had to say, but they also agreed that it would be unproductive to continue to resist. That was the turning point. The rest of the meeting, we were able to focus on possible solutions and agree on a recommendation to move forward. The accusation audit worked.

HOW TO NEGOTIATE OUTCOMES

State the goals and a deadline.
- Before you begin negotiating, set the stage by providing proper context. Everyone in the discussion should be aligned on the objective and understand how making a decision on the topic you are debating will bring you closer to that goal.

Uncover constraints.
- Open the discussion by allowing each person to articulate constraints or concerns.
- Capture constraints and opinions without judgment. Make sure everyone agrees before you start discussing solutions that all of the concerns have been accurately captured.

Outline assumptions.
- Alleviate fears by capturing underlying assumptions for different solutions or estimates that are being provided. This will allow you to move forward, even when there are potential caveats with a solution.

Generate possible solutions.
- Instead of focusing on what cannot be done, spend time focusing on outlining possible solutions.
- Let everyone contribute options to represent all the divergent opinions.
- Discuss pros and cons of each solution.

Make a recommendation or get a tie breaker.
- Once pros and cons exist, coach the group toward a recommendation. Prompt them to review the pros and cons and

to each vote on solutions that best satisfy the constraints and meet the goals.

- If an obvious recommendation does not emerge, seek a tie breaker from your project sponsor to make the final decision.
- If all collaborative negotiation tactics fail, perform an accusation audit by acknowledging all the objections being presented. Then ask your team to accept the mandate to proceed and work collaboratively on defining possible solutions.

Communicate the final decision.

- Capture the final decision in writing.
- Communicate the final decision and the reasons for the final decision.

CHAPTER 13

How to Communicate
What's Most Important

Remember the conductor of the orchestra, the woman who was elegantly standing in front, artfully waving her arms and hands in order to keep each musician in harmony with the others? If you examine her closely, you'll notice she was communicating with every person in the orchestra. She was encouraging each musician, as an expert in their own right. Each musician was playing their own notes for their part of the song, perfectly. She was the force keeping everyone aligned. She was telling each person with her baton exactly what was most important in each moment. She was a beacon, projecting what each player needed to know, at exactly the right time, so that they could play their notes, shine rightfully with their own talent, and partner with her to make beautiful music.

My role as a project leader is akin to the conductor's role for her orchestra. My most critical function is to always be communicating what is most important. I act as a beacon for anyone needing a guide to follow. It's my job to show each person on my team respect—the sponsors, the product owners, the engineers, the designers, the support specialists, the marketers—and I listen to what they say needs to be done, I support them, and then I cue them up when it's their time to act. I focus them on the goal, and I prompt them when to play their part.

Similarly, when you lead projects, you will act as a hub of information with a purpose—to communicate what's most important, to the right audience, at the right time. You find out what is most important by being aligned with your sponsor, then asking your teams what needs to be done to achieve what's most important. Then you synthesize all of that information and communicate it back at exactly the right time. You expedite handoffs to make sure those transitions are seamless when the time is right. Finally, you partner with your team to get it all done. Simple, elegant, but not always easy.

There are two hard skills to master here: First, how do you get enough information to know what's important? People don't always tell you what is important. Sometimes you have to sense it, and sometimes you have to artfully extract it from them. Second, how do you deliver messages to the right audience at the right time in such a way that they hear and understand it?

Not every conductor is able to deliver because the players may not understand her signals. A conductor who waves her arms wildly isn't an effective beacon. The musicians must intuitively understand what she is communicating, and that is where her skill for using the right signal for each audience is tested. That is where communication skills for project leaders are tested as well.

Understand the many ways teams communicate

When a baby is born, you think she only has one way of communicating. She is either silent or she cries. She has no words. Her sight is clouded so you can't read from her eyes if she is terrified or happy. She doesn't even have control of her limbs to point at what upsets her. All she can do is wail when she's uncomfortable, and it's up to you as her parent to learn how to comfort her.

Over time, you learn to read her nonverbal cues—the grimaces she makes on her face, whether her skin is cold or she is sweaty, whether she is restless or calm in your arms. You start to develop an intuition for what she needs based on taking in all her cues, verbal and nonverbal.

Believe it or not, even though we are fully grown adults, we still communicate like infants; the vast majority of our communication is nonverbal. In *The Only Negotiating Guide You'll Ever Need*, the authors devote an entire chapter purely to nonverbal communication because it is so critical for understanding what adults are truly saying.

They said, "Research in communication suggests that as much as 90 percent of the meaning transmitted between two people in face-to-face communications is via nonverbal channels." The most direct way to get information is to ask questions, but that may still only be 10 percent of the information. Beyond listening to words, you need to observe your team to hear the majority of what they are communicating.

When I initially started listening to nonverbal cues, it was difficult to pinpoint exactly what made me feel as if a team was in trouble. But I was pretty good at sensing it. If I trusted my spider senses and probed my team with questions, I would often uncover that there was more to the story than was being told.

Now, I can identify these nonverbal cues more clearly. There are a few that have consistently stood out as key indicators over the course of the hundreds of projects I've seen. First is the volume of questions being posed. A person who asks a reasonable number of questions about his task is working diligently and making progress. That's usually how I know we are on the track. But a person who asks too many questions is likely confused and needs help. A person who asks no questions may have not started yet because he is overloaded or may be blocked. When I notice no questions or too many questions, I'll probe more deeply to understand how I can help.

What is most important to me is helping the team do what is most important now. If the team is not performing well, if tasks are off track, it's my job to communicate what's happening. Everyone else may be so focused on the task at hand that they may not notice. I point them to the most critical task that needs help. A team that owns their responsibilities will recognize the risk and act accordingly. They will use the redundancy we've built into the team to pitch in until the most important tasks are done.

I also watch the time of day when work is getting done. A healthy team will have healthy working hours, take breaks for lunch, and sleep a full night. A person who consistently works through lunch hour or late at night is likely overloaded with work. A person who starts work late and ends work early may be burned out, or on the cusp of burnout. I probe, I communicate the risk, and then again focus them on what's most important. A team will not do well if they do not care for themselves. I communicate when it's critical to push and act with heroism and when it's critical to rest and recover for sanity. It's my job to guard the team from letting their own sense of responsibility trump their health.

The last indicator is team chemistry. I observe how teams are working together and how the room feels when they are working together. A team whose updates at scrum bounce with a certain amount of energy is healthy. A team whose energy is constantly low or angry or vacant needs help. They won't be able to get what's most important done, or they will soon falter. It's my job to ask about what I am noticing and to identify the risk and work with my team and their sponsor to solve it.

By watching for the implicit ways in which my team is communicating with me—through both words and nonverbal cues—I'm able to glean if there are big risks that need to be addressed. I'm able to focus everyone on delivering on what's most important, and ensure the team is healthy enough to do so.

Volume of questions	Time of day when work gets done	Team energy during meetings
Too many questions: The team may be confused and need help.	**Working during lunch or late nights:** Your team may be overloaded.	**Contentious meetings:** Team members may be unsatisfied.
Too few questions: The team may be blocked or delayed from starting work.	**Starting late or leaving early:** Morale may be low or burnout is happening.	**Low participation or energy:** Morale may be low or overloaded.

Cues for understanding team health.

Consistently communicate what's most important

Four items are most important on any project at any given time. These are not in order because all of them are important and must be communicated at all times. The purpose of my day, as I navigate through my packed calendar and my full inbox, is to constantly evaluate and communicate how we are doing on these four items:

- **A sense of purpose:** What is the next milestone leading to your goal, as well as how the work they are doing supports it?
- **The highest impact items:** Which items are the highest impact and require the highest level of focus and priority?
- **Timing:** What is the right time for each person to act?
- **Risk to achieving delivery:** What blockers hinder completion of work or threaten the productivity of your team?

How do I know the answers to these questions? I am aligned with my sponsor so I always know the most important milestone and goal. I listen intently to my team, ask questions, and synthesize their answers. I identify risks based on what they have told me verbally and nonverbally, and I work with them to take action. I mirror instructions that the team has given me, but just on a time delay. My team commits to work and they tell me what needs to be done. I keep them honest by reminding them of their commitments. Finally, I keep track of time and communicate to the most relevant audience at the most relevant point in time.

In a way, it's as if I'm functioning like the team's personal Alexa—they set a reminder with me that goes off at just the right time to cue them into action. At any time, when they are lost, they can ask how much time they have left to do what they've committed to doing, and I will tell them. I am acting as their conductor and their partner.

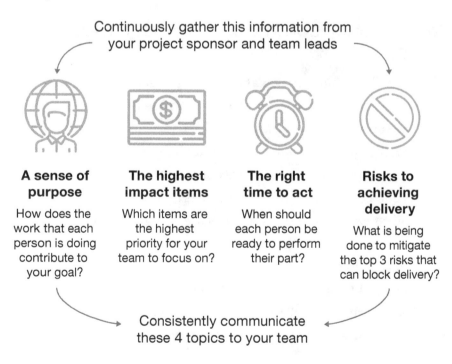

The most important topics to communicate.

Tailor communication to each audience

Why don't teams just use an Alexa then? Because of emotional intelligence. Alexa is a bot; you are a person who cares about leading your team. You can read them and adapt to what they need most. You have the ability to adjust your tone, your delivery, and the information based on your audience, and you will be most effective when you do so at getting people to listen.

When you are leading from the middle of the organization, there are five relative audiences that you must communicate with: executives, sponsors, team leads, individual contributors, and project stakeholders. Each of them requires a slightly different version of you.

When you present to *executives*, you want to present with a respectful yet authoritative tone. Share just the most relevant and interesting business details in order to showcase the team's progress, accomplishments, next milestones, and risks. One of the best pieces of advice I've ever been given when preparing for an executive presentation is that the most impactful presentations are those that are insightful. Pull out nuggets of wisdom, synthesize your updates into a story, and tell the story. No more, no less.

When you communicate with your *sponsor*, there should also be respect in your tone. The best relationship between a sponsor and a project lead is collaborative. Your sponsor focuses you on what's important. You offer advice on how to proceed. You share the same project details as you did with the executives—progress accomplishments, next milestones, and risks—but without any sugarcoating. You also make clear requests when your team needs help.

In *The Gatekeepers* by Chris Whipple, Donald Rumsfeld recounts from his experience as White House chief of staff to Gerald Ford, "Because the chief of staff is with him day in and day out, he has the ability to select moments when he can look at a president and tell him something with the bark off. He is the one person besides his wife who can do that—who can look him right in the eye and say, 'This is not right. You simply can't go down that road. Believe me, it's not going to work, it's a mistake.'"

Like a chief of staff, ultimately, it's your responsibility to support the sponsor who makes the decisions. But when you communicate one-on-one, honesty will go a long way to building trust as well as to create the best collaborative decision-making for your project.

When you communicate with *team leads*, you should feel as if you are as directly responsible as they are to deliver. When you speak with them, speak on behalf of your sponsor, as a delegate to represent the sponsor's views and ensure that decisions are guided by the sponsor's intention. Communicate what is most important now and what will be most important next. Work together to identify risks and overcome challenges. Learn what you can do to help the team to deliver now and to prepare for what is to come. Be confidants with your team leads. They must trust you with their fears and their requests. Working with you, this group will decide how to steer the individual contributors on your team. They will be your fellow conductors for your cause.

Individual contributors are the most earnest group who will be seeking guidance. Your tone with them should be authoritative, helpful, caring, and inspiring. You should constantly connect their daily work to purpose. Be approachable so that they can come to you for help, questions, or advice at any time. Be as detail oriented as needed to give these team members clarity. These are the people who actually get the work done, day in and day out. Communicate to them with the respect, attention, and the level of detail and appreciation they deserve.

Finally, there are *project stakeholders*. These are the people who live on the fringes of your project but will play an important role at some point in time—either because they have a task that your team depends on, or they are impacted downstream by your project. When you communicate with them, be concise, informative, and specific about the piece of work that will require their help. Seek advice on what can be done to prepare them to best do their jobs. Let them know well in advance when they are going to need to perform their piece and then count down as it comes close. Because these people do not live and breathe your project day in and day out, giving them a heads-up well before their time to act will make you most successful in getting their cooperation.

HOW TO TAILOR COMMUNICATION TO EACH AUDIENCE

Communicate daily to your sponsor, your leads, and your team.

- Project Sponsor
  - ☐ When communicating with your sponsor, your stance should always be respectful, informative, and collaborative.
  - ☐ Communicate a non-sugarcoated version of your project— status, progress, upcoming milestones, and risks.
  - ☐ Ask your sponsor for direction, key decisions, and help when you are unable to resolve issues on your own with the team.
- Team Leads
  - ☐ Be anchoring, partnering, trusting when communicating with your team leads.
  - ☐ Communicate intent from project sponsor, potential risks being communicated through both verbal and nonverbal cues from the team.
  - ☐ Remind the team leads of the most important tasks, commitments, and the right time to act.
  - ☐ Collaborate on mitigation plans for blockers and risk.
- Individual Contributors
  - ☐ Aim to be authoritative, helpful, caring, and inspiring when communicating with individual team members.
  - ☐ Communicate how their daily work connects to purpose.
  - ☐ Remind them of the most important tasks, commitments, and the right time to act.

Communicate regularly with other executives and stakeholders.

- Executives
  - ☐ Communicate with confidence and a goal to provide insightful information when reporting out to executives or those higher on the totem pole than you.

- ☐ Share a synthesized story of your project—status, progress, upcoming milestones, and risks.
- ◆ Other project stakeholders
  - ☐ With any other stakeholder who will need to play a role on your project, but is not involved on a daily basis, be concise and informative.
  - ☐ Keep them abreast of a high-level project status and timeline.
  - ☐ Make specific requests that will require work and when.
  - ☐ Seek acknowledgment and commitment that they are willing and will be ready to perform the role that you need them to perform. Ask for feedback on what you can do to best prepare them.
  - ☐ Provide a countdown to when they will need to act and connect handoffs as needed.

CHAPTER 14

When Is Your Project Done? It's Not What You Think

If you've made it to this point in my book, I'd like to applaud your grit and persistence. I have just a few words of advice left for you. You've journeyed with me through all the major phases of your project and soaked up the advice I've had for you to effectively navigate them. All that is left is for you to learn how to finish a project.

I am confident that you will successfully finish your project, as long as you don't make the mistake I almost made when I was writing this book.

When I first started writing this book, I did everything I thought I needed to do to credibly call myself an author. I agonized over what I wanted to write, spent weeks organizing my thoughts, did research to crystallize my thinking, sought creative ways to express my advice, and read books to learn the technical aspects of writing. I carved out time in my schedule and plotted a timeline to get it all done. I focused on the writing, because that's what authors do. They write.

I had glorified in my mind what it meant to be an author. It seemed like a brave, solitary endeavor—one accomplished only through determination and the hunger to write what was in my heart, and to put it out into the world to share with others. When I finished writing my first draft, I was so proud of myself. I felt like I had set out to climb a mountain alone and had made it to the summit.

Then, two months went by and nothing happened. My book collected virtual dust as it sat on my hard drive.

One day, a friend of mine whom I hadn't spoken to since I finished my first draft asked me about the progress of my book. When I heard her question, I winced. At that moment, I realized I was currently on a path to fail. In order to become a successful author, you must publish your book. I had been so focused on writing the book that I had stopped short of the tasks I needed to do to get my book ready to be published. It was a classic mistake, and one I had seen often on other projects. Thankfully, I knew what I needed to do to fix it.

I needed to take full ownership for the success of my book. I needed to stop thinking of myself narrowly as just the author and instead be a project leader.

As soon as I started thinking of myself as the project leader for my book, I knew my job was far from done. I expanded my purview so that I could start to see the remaining tasks I needed to complete to get my book into the hands of readers like you. My research indicated that I needed at least an editor, a book designer, and early readers for my book. I needed to come up with a plan to promote my book after it was available for purchase in the Amazon bookstore. I needed to build an author site so that my readers could connect with me. There was so much more to do that I didn't see until I took full ownership.

The project that started as a solitary endeavor would soon expand to have a team. The shift in my mindset propelled me to take the initiative to find a professional editor and start the next phase of my project. She will help me identify the remaining gaps and locate individuals to help me with them. From this point forward, I know I will not fail because I will not stop until I have all the help I need to successfully finish this project.

In one of my favorite self-help books, *What Happy People Know*, author Dan Baker explains why the words we choose to describe ourselves affect our actions. "We don't describe the world we see—we see the world we describe," he said. "Language, as the single most fundamental force of the human intellect, has the power to alter perception. We think in words, and these words have the power to limit us or to set us free; they can frighten us or evoke our courage. Similarly, the stories we tell ourselves about our own lives eventually become our lives. We can tell healthy stories or horror stories. The choice is ours."

By changing the words I was using to describe my role for my book, I actually freed myself from the limits I was imposing on my thinking. The same method will work for you.

And that is what this short but important chapter is about. I originally decided to add this chapter after I wrote the first draft because I felt there was something missing. All projects have a start and an end. I had written many chapters about laying the foundation for a project but not one about how to end it. I began writing this with the intention of sharing tips on how to finish a project. But then I quickly realized that there was no blueprint I would be able to share that would guarantee you would finish your projects every time. The secret to consistently finishing projects has more to do with how you think about your role on the project, and what you do with that role than what you are assigned to do.

Angela Duckworth, the Rosa Lee and Egbert Chang Professor of Psychology at the University of Pennsylvania, has done extensive research on the psychology of success. In her book *Grit*, Duckworth shares an interesting study conducted by Warren Willingham in 1978 who sought to identify traits that were the best predictors of success in adulthood. Willingham's findings: "Follow-through was the single best predictor of holding an appointed or elected leadership position in young adulthood. And, finally, better than any of the more than one hundred personal characteristics Willingham had measured, follow-through predicted notable accomplishments for a young adult in all domains, from the arts and writing to entrepreneurism and community service."

Similarly, your ability to take ownership of your project and follow through on doing whatever you need to do in order to lead it to success will be your best predictor for success.

For every project, there is the place you thought it might end and there is the point at which it actually ends. For my book, I thought writing the book would get me to the end. It turned out that I had a lot more to do to get my book published, including writing this chapter.

For product development projects, we often think the launch date is the end, but there is much more beyond that. You need to deal with issues as they arise post-launch. You need to handle all of the road-kill that you cut along the way to the launch. You need to transition your project to those who will support it. You need to train others to use it. Each project is different, so it's difficult to define exactly what you need to do. As long as you feel like you own the project, you will conjure the grit to work through those tasks as they arise, and you will find a way to complete them. That's what project leaders do. And that's what you will do.

You must see yourself as a leader and have a sense of ownership for your project end to end. When you feel like you own a project, you naturally do what it takes until the project is finished. You don't stop when you hit a blockage, you work through it. You don't stop when the scope of the role you were assigned stops. You look downstream from your role, beyond what you may already know. You uncover what needs to be done, you make no excuses, you follow-through and you do it.

Now, instead of relying on a how-to section at the end of this chapter, try this—discard your current title and claim that of a project leader. Take ownership for your project. Then, take a moment now to reflect on the original point you had in your mind for its end. It may have been the completion of a chapter like this one, a draft, an initial plan, a phase of development, a launch date. Can you see beyond the horizon? You have more work to do to get to the end of the road, and you see it now. That is the path you will take and lead to the finish.

CHAPTER 15

You Already Know How to Lead Change. Embrace It

When I was pregnant with my first child, I thought I'd be able to "project manage" my way into motherhood. It worked for my wedding, it worked when I had to move across the country, it worked at my job. Why couldn't it work for a baby?

If you are a parent, I'm sure you are already chuckling inside because you know how the story ends. That approach didn't work. I read a big pile of parenting books, bought lots of sophisticated baby gadgets, and imagined how I would train my baby girl to the perfect daily schedule—one that would allow me to catch enough sleep and also be productive during my maternity leave. I was naive.

My little girl had other plans. She came into the world with a big spirit. She had a lot of emotions and wasn't afraid to express them. She cried incessantly when she was unhappy, and she was unhappy often. And then there were times (about five minutes at a time, to be exact) of pure joy, when her little smile would light up the world. She didn't follow a schedule. She nursed more often than other babies. She wanted her diaper changed more often. She woke five times a night. She would only nap in my arms, while I was sitting on a yoga ball, bouncing, so I did that for about eight hours a day, every day, for the first six weeks of her life. I was not in the least productive. I did not sleep. There was no way to manage her.

Then one day, she suddenly seemed calm and happy, and she slept a five-hour stretch. I felt like a pro. I thought, "Mama, you're good at this, you can do this." But then just as I began to feel comfortable, she changed again.

Babies are always changing and growing. Each week, they acquire a new superpower. They start to see further, have more control over their muscles. They start to learn language, how to roll, and sit, and crawl, and stand. At around nine months, they learn that they are not the same person as their parents and they flip out royally. My baby was always changing, and the only way to manage her was to *not* manage her. I learned that lesson the hard way. When I freaked out from change, she would freak out even more. I had to adjust and expect that change would come, and then adjust again until we found something that fit for just that moment. It was when I started anticipating change that I became calmer, and she became calmer and happier as well.

Projects are similar to babies. There is no project I've ever led that has gone as planned. No matter how hard you try to manage or control them, change will happen. And while projects might not be quite as volatile or as stressful as becoming a new parent, they can feel pretty darn close.

Managing is for things, but projects are delivered by people. People come and go. They learn new skills and change their minds, then they change their minds back. They get promoted. They get sick. They go on leave. They get demoralized, and then inspired. They become tired, and then they find energy. Leading projects is about leading people, and because people are always changing, so are your projects.

The concept of impermanence from Buddhist philosophy provides insightful guidance for dealing with change. Noah Rasheta, a Buddhist teacher, explains in his book *No-Nonsense Buddhism for Beginners*: "The nature of reality is that all things are constantly changing, and therefore all things are impermanent. Jobs, relationships, good times, bad times, our thoughts and feelings, our loved ones, our own selves—literally everything as we know or perceive it—will pass out of existence. The problem is that even if we know this, we continue to cling to things as if they were permanent because we want them to last."

Human beings like to believe that things are permanent when, in fact, they are not. That is one of the major causes of our suffering. It's the expectation of permanence that actually causes us grief. It's the clash between the expectation that we can control something and the reality that we cannot.

We can't prevent change, even when we want things to stay the same. So the best course of action is to embrace it.

John P. Kotter, the Konosuke Matsushita Professor of Leadership, Emeritus, at the Harvard Business School, argues that successful change also requires the leadership team to adapt quickly and fully. Leaders who fail to do this will also cause their teams to fail. In his book *Leading Change*, he said, "Perhaps worst of all are supervisors who refuse to adapt to new circumstances and who make demands that are inconsistent with the transformation." You cannot expect teams to change if you do not change yourself. You need to provide clear direction through your own actions.

To successfully lead change, you have to embrace change on your projects just like I embraced change with my baby girl. You must anticipate it and stay calm when it happens so that when your team looks at you, they know it'll be okay. And then you must demonstrate to others how they should adapt.

The good news is that you do not need to learn additional skills to lead change. All projects are change. Leading change at the beginning, the middle, or at end of a project requires the same set of skills. Since you've already learned those skills throughout this book, you simply need to apply them to help your team navigate change, no matter what phase it happens during your project.

Let's review how you can lead change, as a final lesson to demonstrate your newfound mastery for leading projects.

Change happens. What are the next steps?

- You ask questions to understand the reason for the change, synthesize what and who it will impact, and codify it in writing.
- You revise the goals to make them unambiguous under the new landscape.
- You work with your sponsor and your team leads to realign the work in flight to your new goals.
- You ask more questions and synthesize what the change will impact.
- You communicate the new goals and changes directly, honestly, and broadly through a well-planned meeting to the project team at large.
- You uncover possible solutions for how to proceed and negotiate agreeable outcomes.
- You reprioritize features and rebalance scope, time, and resources.
- You identify and preempt new risks.
- You act as a beacon by repeating the new goals in every medium to every audience.
- You extract what needs to be done to adjust to the new goals. You anchor the team on what is important, cue them up when it's time for them to play their part, and connect their daily work to purpose.
- You encourage your team, you rally around them, you listen to their concerns, you fill gaps, you bubble up risks.
- You support your team through the change as they need support, by going above and beyond your role to fill any gaps you see.
- Then when change happens again, you rinse and repeat.

And so it goes until your project is finished. Then you plan a big launch party for your team. You celebrate because you guided your team, you trusted them, and, together, you got the job done.

Change happens on every project. What defines your success is how you react to it. Will you jump toward it with your arms wide open, ready to show your teams how to follow? Or will you recoil into a world of checklists and status reports for comfort? I think you will act as the first follower and embrace it. I think you will be brave enough to trust your teammates and relinquish control. I think you will act like an owner to march your team successfully to the finish line of your project. I think you will do your part to support them and act as their partner, their conductor, their pilot, their beacon, their friend, their project leader.

You will be the connective tissue that binds your team together and leads them to success. You will guide them, and they will follow.

Get Started

Build Rapport		
Ask Effective Questions	Run Productive Meetings	Take Great Notes
Synthesize Information		

Lay a Solid Foundation

Create Alignment	Plan When Your Team Needs It	Preempt Risk	Personalize the Process

Support Your Project In Flight

Communicate What's Most Important		
Expedite Handoffs	Negotiate Outcomes	Manage Trade-offs
Embrace Change		

Summary of how to lead projects.

PART IV

How to Make Work More Than a Project

CHAPTER 16

What Motivates Me Every Time I Set Foot in the Office

I work a lot. When I'm working on a big project, I am fully dedicated to its success so I do whatever it takes to get the job done. As a result, it's not uncommon for me to spend sixty hours a week working. I spend more time working than any other singular activity—I spend more time working than I do enjoying leisure time with my family, more time than on any hobby, more time than fulfilling my basic physical needs for exercise, eating, and sleeping. For something to take up that much space in my life, it has to mean a lot to me.

Ironically though, I've never been driven by any specific company mission. I'm not the person that Ticketmaster hired to sell the most tickets, that Opower hired to save the most energy, or that Edmunds hired to help people buy cars more easily. Who I am, however, is a person who can find a meaningful role at any thriving company.

What motivates me most is not company-specific, but the genuine desire to help the people I share most of my time with. I am loyal to my coworkers. They are people I care about—people whom I've developed partnerships with, solved big problems with, wept with, hugged. My bond with them is what drives me to put as much of myself into my work as possible, and it's what makes every hour I spend working worth it.

In their article from Gallup.com, "Your Friends and Your Social Well-Being," Tom Rath and Jim Harter share a similar sentiment that having strong relationships at work is inherently motivating. "We spend more of our waking hours at work than at home, and it's only natural that we want to build connections with our team members. We want work to feel worthwhile and having trusted confidants and supporters helps foster that feeling. We go to our work friends when we need to celebrate and commiserate about our personal and professional lives. In the absence of that outlet, work can seem lonely and isolating. It lacks attachments. We may like what we do, we may get to use our talents and strengths every day, but we're probably not feeling fully energized or motivated to put our whole selves into our roles."

Because spending time with people I care about is what drives me, the result is that my greatest relationships in life also read like a trail of my work history. I met my best friend of over twenty years when I was working in IT consulting. I met my husband when I was working at Ticketmaster. Even though Derrek and I were married after we had both left Ticketmaster, our wedding was flooded by Ticketmaster alums, several who were in our wedding party. The same alums attended the baby shower for our first child three years later. Similarly, my ten years at Edmunds has left me with so many great friendships that they would be hard to count.

I am confident that the greatest project leaders are those who have forged bonds with their teams similar to mine. They are the ones who—with appreciation, empathy, encouragement, trust, loyalty, and strength—from plans and goals, create work friends and work families.

They are social centers of teams. Instead of focusing solely on task planning and status reports, they also use their organizational prowess to plan launch celebrations, holiday potlucks, any-reason potlucks, baby showers. They take photos. They send group birthday cards and welcome-to-your-first-day notes. They collect farewell wishes when a teammate leaves. They sing and dance and drink with those left behind. They are the ones who take up gift collections when a member of the team is grieving.

They appreciate good, hard work and say "thank you."

They listen and empathize and ask, "How can I help?"

They shine the spotlight on those who have been working quietly, loyally, and diligently and deserve recognition.

They measure their success based on both delivery and team happiness. They celebrate with pride when the team wins, because a win for the team is a win for themselves.

Ultimately, they treat work like it is more than a job; they use work as a way to enrich lives by creating lasting relationships and lasting memories. And they spawn a positive culture for their teams from doing so.

Do I do these? I absolutely do. In fact, when I received a peer-nominated award at Edmunds for my work, they described me as "the chair of our unofficial birthday committee" who has the added responsibility of "remembering everyone's snack preferences" and is a person "who has the ability to make every team member feel valued." Those are the types of compliments I cherish most because they are evidence that people know how much I care.

When I treat my work relationships like friendships, it transforms my entire outlook. Work is not just a job, but a way to accomplish amazing things with amazing friends. It becomes less about what I am doing, and more about who I'm doing it with. That perspective motivates me every time I set foot in the office.

During my research for this book, I also found overwhelming evidence that being happy, connected, working at a place where people care about you, and having genuine friendships makes you more productive. As a result, strengthening bonds among team members creates more effective teams. As Matt Mochary writes in *The Great CEO*

Within, "It turns out that we perform our best when we are having fun and feeling good about ourselves."

Similarly, Shawn Achor shares in his book *The Happiness Advantage,* "Countless studies have found that social relationships are the best guarantee of heightened well-being and lowered stress, both an antidote for depression and a prescription for high performance."

In her article on Gallup.com, "Why We Need Best Friends at Work," Annamarie Mann reinforces my experience that making *best* friends at work has many benefits too. "Our research revealed that just 30 percent of employees have a best friend at work. Those who do are seven times as likely to be engaged in their jobs, are better at engaging customers, produce higher quality work, have higher well-being, and are less likely to get injured on the job. In sharp contrast, those without a best friend in the workplace have just a 1 in 12 chance of being engaged." My best friend may not always realize it, but she's a big reason why I work so hard and stay so engaged. I feel supported because she is near, and my work has more meaning because I can share it with her.

Being connected at work, having friends, and best friends at work, makes me happier. It makes work fun and more rewarding. It fills me with greater purpose than just achieving a goal for a company. It makes my time at work more meaningful. I'm sharing an experience with people I care about, with people who care about me too.

*   *   *

On January 7, 2020, Edmunds conducted a round of layoffs that was exceptionally difficult for our familial culture. In an effort to be as transparent as possible under the circumstances, the company leadership had announced that layoffs were coming several days before it happened. However, due to the sensitive nature of the events, the names of those affected were not revealed until that day.

I began mourning the moment I heard the news. I knew we would all feel a deep sense of loss no matter who would be leaving us.

Before we knew exactly who would go and who would stay, I decided to organize a "come whatever your fate, not-so-happy hour" at a small bar nearby. My coworkers and I flooded the bar when the layoffs were done that Tuesday afternoon so that we could all be together one last time. We hugged, we laughed, we ate terrible pizza, we drank, we said farewell to many. We commiserated with those who were staying. It was epic, it was fun, it was hard, and it was healing.

The next day, I felt as if I had been run over by a truck, had it back up over me, and then run over me again. I was so relieved to survive. Then that evening at 11:30 p.m. I received an unexpected call from my mom. My dad was in the hospital.

I spent the majority of my free time for the next sixteen days by my father's side in the critical care unit. In his last five days, he lost consciousness and was intubated. I was there every morning at seven and retired after eight in the evening. I abandoned a critical project at work that was marching toward its launch and no one batted an eye. The owner of the company even sent me a message to tell me not to worry about work and to take as much time as I needed to be with my family. I did.

On Friday, January 23, 2020, my father passed away while my sister and I held his hands and sang to him.

Though I was grieving, I decided not to take any additional time off work and returned to the office the following Monday. As soon as I walked through the office doors, a friend and coworker sprinted toward me and wrapped me in her arms. She whispered, "I'm so sorry. Are you okay to be here?" I teared up and nodded slowly.

She looked me in the eyes and said, "I'm here for you," and then let go so that I could proceed with my day. All day, my coworkers gently reminded me that it was okay to go home, but I refused because I wanted to stay. I wanted to be with the work family I had built for myself. I wanted a distraction and I wanted support when I was not distracted. I didn't want to be at home with my thoughts and my big emotions.

In the coming days and weeks, I broke down and cried in front of a number of my coworkers, my friends. I got big hugs when I needed them. I sat in meetings with a lump in my throat and dismissed myself when I needed time. I found private spaces to sit quietly when I needed to be alone. My work family sent me sympathy cards, flowers, a cactus plant (because they know I am a houseplant killer). They offered condolences both openly and silently by picking up slack for me at work when I needed it. They sent flowers to my father's funeral service and contributed to charities in his name. I never said thank you. It was too painful and I didn't know what to say. I didn't need to say it. They did it because they cared for me and, after all of the times that I had supported them, I selfishly accepted their support when I needed it.

In the same way I counted on them, everyone on my team knows they can count on me when we face new challenges during a project or when a big event disrupts their lives. They know because they are my friends. And that is what makes us both a high-performing team and a work family.

One of the most impactful books I've read that has helped me understand why the strong relationships I've built at work are so important to me is *Grit* by Angela Duckworth. As Duckworth writes, "But the magic of culture is that one person's grit can provide a model for others . . . one person's grit enhances the grit of others, which in turn inspires more grit in that person, and so on without end."

In the end, what means the most to me is that how I lead my projects has a significant and positive impact on the culture for my entire team. Similar to how grit can be self-renewing, the actions I take to cultivate a workplace where I care about my coworkers and build lasting friendships, creates a cycle that ensures the people on my team will do the same.

There is no how-to section for this chapter because you already know how to do it.

Care. Ask questions about life and listen. Share yourself. Appreciate. Give support, take support. Be honest. Be brave. Make friends, make best friends. Have fun and laugh with your friends. Cry and be sad with your friends. Heal together with your friends.

Where there once was just a project, create a family, create a community.

Be a leader. Be the glue. Be you.

Acknowledgments:
To All the People Who Helped Me Fulfill this Dream

I have dreamed of writing a book ever since I was in college, but I never truly pursued a path to make it happen until COVID-19 hit. Somehow, during one of the most challenging years of my life—in the wake of losing my father and amid a pandemic—all the stars aligned to give me the time, inspiration, resources, and determination to get it done. I am in utter disbelief that I've finally been able to make this dream come true.

But like all of my big projects, I didn't do it alone. I had a team of people who supported me at home, at work, and in virtual communities. I'd like to take a moment to thank all those folks here for the integral roles they have played in my life and in this book.

First and foremost, to my husband, Derrek Long, thank you for not looking at me like I was insane when I told you I wanted to write a book. Thank you for distracting the kids with video games on the many evenings when I was writing, taking field trips on the weekends when I was editing, and for being a sounding board when I needed to work out some of my thoughts. Without you, this book certainly would not exist.

To my kids, Maile and Lio, thank you for the endless interruptions. There is no better way to interrupt the writing process than with hug breaks, or to receive a piece of artwork that can be taped to the wall by my desk. (I could have done without interruptions that involved poop, but you have to accept and love the whole package when it comes to you.) I hope that this book makes you proud of your mama someday when you're old enough to read it.

To my mom, Christine Thuy Pham, and my sister, Mai Pham, you didn't even know I was writing this book because I wasn't sure if I'd make it and I wanted to surprise you when it was finished. You have both been role models for me as I've grown. I did it for you, to make you proud, and for everything you did to make my childhood easy. I did it for Dad too.

To my very best friends, Julie Woo, Richard Tang, and Sam Lu. In my life, I never receive anything but unconditional support and encouragement from the three of you. You are family to me.

To Edmunds, for giving me the opportunity to work on interesting projects, the time to work on this book, a wonderful community of coworkers, and for allowing me to publish what I learned while working with them. I am grateful to have worked for a company that has granted me so many interesting opportunities in my career.

To Eugene Park and Nick Gorton, I am lucky to have you both as role models and mentors. It has been a privilege to work with such strong leaders. I'm sure you saw yourselves several times throughout this book. What I've learned from you has been so integrated into my body of thinking that your advice echoes in my mind anytime I'm facing a challenge.

To my friends and coworkers (past and present) who wrote back when I asked for words of encouragement: Holly Dudley, Shawn Kim, Jeff Kolesky, Sean Owen, Andrew Wang, Dori Merifield, Renwick Oden, Martina Banev, Maya Palmer, and Clara Kim. I kept those words close when I was writing the book and called on them for inspiration. Thank you for sending such thoughtful responses. (To those who didn't write back, I love you anyway.)

To those who attended my project management courses at "Edmunds University," thank you for showing me that I had advice to give that could be helpful to others. You may not know it, but you inspired me to write this book.

To all my other coworkers at Edmunds, Opower, and Ticketmaster, if you saw a glimpse of yourself in this book, thank you. I would not have written a line if it weren't for all the times that I learned valuable lessons working with you.

To the many other friends and coworkers—there are too many to name—who told me they would be excited to read my book when I shared the news that I was going to write it. Whether you were genuinely excited or feigned your excitement to spare my feelings, I appreciate it. When you write, you have no idea if anyone will want to read it, and hearing those words from others definitely helps to quiet the skepticism that creeps into your thoughts while you are writing.

To authors William Zinsser and Stephen King for your books on the writing process, *On Writing Well* and *On Writing*, respectively. Your timeless advice helped me, as an aspiring writer, gain more confidence about choosing the right words to share my thoughts.

To all of the authors of the many books that I quoted throughout this book, all of whom are identified in the References section, thank you for sharing your knowledge with the world. Not only did you give me valuable advice that I'm able to apply to make myself better at my job, you gave me the supporting content I needed to make my own story stronger with your expertise.

To my wonderful beta and early readers: Joy Shin, Michael Lu-Jones, Steven Hwang, Erin Claybaugh, Gena Urowsky, Satish Chilakala, Michelle Wong, Joseph Siu, Martina Banev, Ashley Daum and Jacob Masga. Thank you for your candid feedback and perspective as readers. I am ever appreciative and humbled that you invested your time to make my book better.

Thank you, Sandra Wendel, for agreeing to be my editor and giving genuinely useful, candid, and practical advice to bring this project to fruition. I soaked up all the wonderful tips from your book *Cover to Cover: What First-Time Authors Need to Know about Editing* and also used it as an example for how to organize my own book. The "First-Time Authors Club" Facebook group you moderate also introduced me to a community of authors facing the same questions and struggles as I have. Your help has been invaluable.

To each person who endorsed this book, I reached out to you because you are someone I greatly admire. I truly cannot express how much it means to me to have your praise printed in the pages of this book preceding mine. Thank you.

To Dr. Robert Cialdini, a very special thank you for the generosity with your time, advice, and the amazing endorsement for my book. The timeless insights you share in your book *Influence* have had a significant impact on my approach to leadership (as I've shared in this book). I was honored that you read my writing and was equally stunned to receive your words of encouragement. I am such a fan!

To Michelle Gorton Boss and Dan Silver at MIGO design, thank you for the creativity you brought to the cover design process. I struggled through many versions to find the perfect cover. You did a wonderful job bringing my ideas to life in a way that was far better than anything I could have created myself.

Thank you Meghan Day Healey for your patience and your work designing the interior and finalizing the cover. I'm sure it was challenging working through my questions and feedback. I'm very excited about the final product and can't wait to get it in the hands of readers.

Finally, thank you G&D Media for taking a chance on me as a first-time author. When I set out to write *Glue*, I never imagined that my book would be published by a reputable publisher with a long history of success in the industry. I am truly honored that you chose to invest in me and my book. With your support, I have faith that this book will make it into the hands of many readers and that the advice I have shared will help others find success and fulfillment leading projects in their own workplaces.

References

Books, Talks, and Other Resources That Were Invaluable to Me in the Writing of this Book

Introduction

The Servant: A Simple Story about the True Essence of Leadership, James C. Hunter

Extreme Ownership: How U.S. Navy SEALs Lead and Win, Jacko Willink and Leif Babin

The 7 Habits of Highly Effective People, Stephen Covey

Peopleware: Productive Projects and Teams, Tom DeMarco and Timothy Lister

"Great Teams Need Glue to Hold Together," Don Yaeger, Forbes.com, July 14, 2016

Chapter 1: The Magical Candy Bowl, and Other Tricks to Build Rapport Quickly

How to Win Friends & Influence People, Dale Carnegie

Influence: The Psychology of Persuasion, Robert Cialdini

The Great CEO Within: The Tactical Guide to Company Building, Matt Mochary

The Happiness Advantage: How a Positive Brain Fuels Success in Work and Life, Shawn Achor

Chapter 2: Be a Hero—Run Productive Meetings

Atlassian: You Waste a Lot of Time at Work Infographic

"The Science and Fiction of Meetings," *MIT Sloan Management Review*, December 2007

"I survived another meeting that should have been an email," mugs gift, amazon.com

Why Work Sucks and How to Fix It: The Results-Only Revolution, Cali Ressler and Jody Thompson

"15 Methods of Every Effective Public Speaker," Forbes Coaches Council, Forbes.com, November 2017

Chapter 3: The Essential Questions to Ask to Get Any Project Moving

"The Surprising Power of Questions," Alison Wood Brooks and Leslie K. John, *Harvard Business Review*, May–June 2018

How to Win Friends & Influence People, Dale Carnegie

Influence: The Psychology of Persuasion, Robert Cialdini

The Happiness Advantage: How a Positive Brain Fuels Success in Work and Life, Shawn Achor

Chapter 5: Every Successful Leader Synthesizes Information. You Can Too

American Heritage Dictionary of the English Language

Reading with Meaning: Teaching Comprehension in the Primary Grades, Debbie Miller

Chapter 6: Create Alignment—It's The Best Way to Motivate Your Team

The Gatekeepers: How the White House Chiefs of Staff Define Every Presidency, Chris Whipple

Adventure in Hawaii: Mountain Tubing Adventure

The Seven Dawns of the Aumakua: The Ancestral Spirit Tradition of Hawaii, Moke Kupihea

"How to Start a Movement," Derek Sivers, TED Talk

The Power of Moments: Why Certain Experiences Have Extraordinary Impact, Chip Heath and Dan Heath

Chapter 7: Does Every Project Need a Plan? Nope, Planning Is Optional

The Power of Moments: Why Certain Experiences Have Extraordinary Impact, Chip Heath and Dan Heath

Chapter 8: How to Safely Jump Out of a Plane (Tips for Preempting Risk)

"Job Burnout: How to Spot It and Take Action," Mayo Clinic staff

Solve for Happy: Engineer Your Path to Joy, Mo Gawdat

"Performing a Project Premortem," Gary Klein, *Harvard Business Review*, September 2007

Chapter 9: Why "One-Size-Fits-All" Processes Backfire

Tribe of Mentors: Short Life Advice from the Best in the World, Timothy Ferriss

Forming, Storming, Norming, and Performing, MindTools.com

Group Development, Wikipedia.org

The Servant: A Simple Story about the True Essence of Leadership, James C. Hunter

Chapter 10: How Relay Races Are Won (Hint: It's in the Handoffs)

Great Boss Dead Boss, Ray Immelman

34 Things You Need to Give Up to Be Successful, Benjamin Hardy, *Inc.*

A Wrinkle in Time, Madeleine L'Engle

The Hard Thing about Hard Things: Building a Business When There Are No Easy Answers, Ben Horowitz

Chapter 11: Three Levers to Keep Your Project On Time and On Budget

"Steve Jobs: Here's What Most People Get Wrong about Focus,"
    Zameena Mejia, CNBC, October 2, 2018

Chapter 12: Negotiate Like a Pro, Even If You Hate Negotiating

The Only Negotiating Guide You'll Ever Need, Peter B. Stark and
    Jane Flaherty

Never Split the Difference: Negotiating as If Your Life Depended on It,
    Chris Voss with Tahl Raz

"Weird, or Just Different?" Derek Sivers, TED Talk

The Great CEO Within: The Tactical Guide to Company Building,
    Matt Mochary

Chapter 13: How to Communicate What's Most Important

The Only Negotiating Guide You'll Ever Need, Peter B. Stark and
    Jane Flaherty

*The Gatekeepers: How the White House Chiefs of Staff Define Every
    Presidency*, Chris Whipple

Chapter 14: When Is Your Project Done? It's Not What You Think

What Happy People Know, Dan Baker and Cameron Stauth

Grit: The Power of Passion and Perseverance, Angela Duckworth

Chapter 15: You Already Know How to Lead Change. Embrace It

No-Nonsense Buddhism for Beginners, Noah Rasheta

Leading Change, John P. Kotter

Chapter 16: What Motivates Me Every Time I Set Foot in the Office

The Great CEO Within: The Tactical Guide to Company Building,
    Matt Mochary

*The Happiness Advantage: How a Positive Brain Fuels Success in
    Work and Life*, Shawn Achor

"Why We Need Best Friends at Work," Annamarie Mann, Gallup.com, January 15, 2018

"Your Friends and Your Social Well-Being," Tom Rath and Jim Harter, Gallup.com, August 19, 2010

Grit: The Power of Passion and Perseverance, Angela Duckworth

Thank You for Reading My Book

Despite having deep experience leading all kinds of projects in my career, I found writing this book to be one of the most challenging projects I've ever undertaken. Being a project of only one person doesn't make your task any easier. You have to be organized and goal focused. You have to be kind to yourself but also tough. You have to find unrelenting motivation to keep yourself going when the goal seems too far out of sight and out of reach. And you can't skip any steps.

I started by funding the book with my own time and money, and then aligning myself with the sponsor (me) by creating a goal to have a draft ready to hand off to an editor by my forty-fourth birthday. I formed an initial plan by plastering my bedroom walls with hundreds of Post-it notes, in an effort to turn the mush that was in my brain into a clear storyline. The first milestone I set to finish planning and start writing, I blew past by a week. When I hit the end of my second week, I stopped procrastinating and forced myself to put my virtual pen to paper even though I still didn't feel quite ready to start.

I had holes in my research for the book, knew little about self-publishing, and also had no experience writing a book. Yes, I had good grades in my high school English literature class, and I could quickly summarize the bejesus out of any subject at work, but I didn't know how to write a good book. I diligently documented the questions that needed to be answered and chased them down one by one. I had to be resourceful and seek knowledge from experts. I joined Facebook groups with editors, self-published authors, and consumed twelve books on the topics of self-publishing, writing, and leadership in the first month. I chased down as many answers as I could as quickly as possible. I took great notes and organized a catalog of answers, supporting research, and inspiration.

About 13,000 words into my first draft, I threw myself a curveball when I hit a block. I was brainstorming book titles one night and realized that my initial book concept would not work because I couldn't find a way to express it concisely. The next morning, I rebooted the entire book, rearranged the Post-it notes for every chapter, and then started again from page one. I compressed my timeline and reset the goals to accommodate the loss from my unrealized progress up to that point.

I negotiated with myself to prioritize my work—topics that would stay in or out of the book, or eventually become roadkill as I came closer to finishing the draft. I freed up more time to write by clearing other projects off my plate, in an effort to write more and faster. After pushing myself much harder, I had to adjust my assumptions about how many hours I could practically write in a day so that I could prevent myself from burning out. I used a word count to unambiguously track the progress I was making and fine-tuned my estimates as I learned more about what I was capable of achieving.

I repeated my goals to myself daily and forced myself to constantly prioritize writing the book over other activities that threatened to take me off course—the snacks in my cupboard beckoning me to take another break, the constant notifications on my phone to check social media, the sunshine calling me to go rollerblading at the beach, the newly released trashy romance novel that was calling my name.

I had to take accountability for the book end to end. If a ball was dropped, there was no one to blame except for me. I fueled myself with my own candy bowl and took meals at my desk. I patted myself on the back when I wrote a chapter that just seemed to work. I showed myself appreciation by buying myself Oreo McFlurries when I hit my target word counts. About halfway through the book, I relinquished control and abandoned my outline as I started trusting instincts and the chapters started to write themselves.

I sought advice and words of encouragement from friends and past coworkers and current coworkers to support me. They made me feel I was not alone, that I was part of a community that would celebrate alongside me when I finally held the finished book in my hands.

Now that we are at the end, you are seeing the synthesis of all my work. These are the final thoughts connecting the dots from every conversation, every detail no matter how seemingly insignificant, and every choice I made through the course of this book-writing journey. You have witnessed my embryonic idea evolve into its final form. You have been with me through my struggle to merge individual words into sentences, sentences into paragraphs, and paragraphs into stories that have taken you from page one to the end. As you read these last words, we are celebrating my project launch together.

I'd like to thank you for being a part of my journey by simply reading this book. Whether you are leading your next project at work, planning a wedding, or endeavoring to write your own book, my hope is that the lessons I've shared will help you successfully lead any project you have invited into your life in the same way they helped me.

*   *   *

Before I leave you, I'd like to share one last thought. Earlier in the book, I stressed the importance of sharing yourself with your projects—your thoughts, your feelings, your friendship, whatever you're comfortable sharing with your coworkers that is authentically you. Sharing your unique personality traits with your team is one way to cultivate positive team culture. And those traits don't have to be just organizational or business related. You can use your unique talents to infuse your team with personality as well.

I love music, poetry, and singing (karaoke, not professionally). I discovered a few years into my career that I could merge those loves with my projects by writing clever jingles about work. The jingles I penned became a creative means to show my pride when my project teams achieved a major milestone. After each jingle was written, I recruited a few willing singers to learn the lyrics so that we could unveil it during a celebratory event. When I couldn't find willing singers, I paid my nine-year-old daughter two dollars to sing with me.

These jingles are admittedly quirky, but they are uniquely me. And whether or not my coworkers admit that they like them, our jingle performances always garner hearty applause. Your unique talent is likely not jingle writing, but something else. A cartoonist might create avatars of her teammates for a team portrait. A drummer might recruit teammates for a band. A talented ping pong player might organize a ping pong league. An amateur chef might make potlucks a team ritual. Whatever it is that brings you pleasure outside of work, share some of it. You'll be surprised at the result. And when you look back, you might find that you are as proud of those quirky contributions to your projects as you were about hitting your milestones.

When you give of yourself to your projects, it makes your work exponentially more fulfilling. On the flip side, it also makes it tough to say farewell when your time together is done.

As I write the last words for this section, I'm moved by how much we have both invested in these pages together. Whether or not we know each other personally, we have connected our thoughts and passions through this book and I am now finding it difficult to say goodbye.

This final passage is an excerpt from the jingle I sent to my coworkers at Opower when I left the company in 2010. I can think of no way more fitting for us to part ways than sharing these silly and heartfelt words with you. I hope you have enjoyed our time together learning about yourself and me, and I sincerely hope you will keep in touch.

(To the tune of "Old MacDonald Had a Farm")

Anh Dao Pham bids you farewell,
Auf Wiedersehen, Goodbye!

It's been so great to work with you,
So much, I cannot lie!

With some memories here
And some laughter there
Lots and lots of good friends
Here our friendship does not end

Anh Dao Pham bids you farewell,
Please keep in touch. Goodbye!

To read more of my quirky jingles, please visit www.glueleaders .com/jingles.

Please also connect with me at www.glueleaders.com/contact. I look forward to hearing from you!

About the Author

Anh Dao Pham was born in Sacramento, California, the youngest child of Vietnamese immigrants and the first native-born United States citizen in her family. When Anh was in first grade, her teacher sent home her report card with a note that read, "She could be President someday!" Her parents never forgot it.  Anh was always encouraged to reach high and to take leadership roles in school and work.

Anh (pronounced like *Ann*) graduated as valedictorian from Bella Vista High. She received a BS in math/applied science (cum laude) from the University of California, Los Angeles where she was also a calculus tutor. After college, Anh worked for Fortune 500 companies as an information technology consultant at Deloitte Consulting and eLoyalty. She delivered over one hundred projects for Ticketmaster, including integration projects with iTunes, Major League Baseball, and American Express. She was an early hire at Opower, a green-tech start-up that later IPO'd and was acquired by Oracle.

Anh is currently Vice President, Product & Program Management at Edmunds. She has been integral to virtually every major product development initiative in the last ten years, including the projects that led to the acquisition of CarCodeSMS by Edmunds (2014) and the acquisition of Edmunds by CarMax (2021). She was the recipient of two peer-nominated awards for her work—the Edmunds V12 Award (2013) and a Blueboard Award (2017). At her ten-year anniversary, Anh was described as someone who exemplifies servant leadership. "So while her list of personal accomplishments is impressive," her boss shared, "you will never see her shine the spotlight on herself. So it is fitting that what she is best known for at Edmunds has been the consistent ability to help those around her achieve at their highest potential."

Anh is an avid reader (romance, self-help, and business) and has a goal to read a book a week. On the weekends, you can find her rollerblading at the beach, gallivanting at amusement parks with her kids, and cooking Vietnamese soups so that she can host dinners for family and friends. Anh is also a certified yoga instructor who is registered with Yoga Alliance. She lives with her husband and two children in Los Angeles, California.

CPSIA information can be obtained
at www.ICGtesting.com
Printed in the USA
JSHW041817030222
22503JS00004B/4